THE BOOK OF SLEEP

THE ARAB LIST

Haytham El Wardany

THE BOOK OF SLEEP

TRANSLATED BY ROBIN MOGER

LONDON NEW YORK CALCUTTA

SERIES EDITOR
Hosam Aboul-Ela

Seagull Books, 2021

First published in Arabic as *Kitab Al Nawm*
by Haytham El Wardany

© Al Karma Publishers, Cairo, 2017

First published in English by Seagull Books, 2020

English translation © Robin Moger, 2020

ISBN   978 0 8574 2 953 7

British Library Cataloguing-in-Publication Data

A catalogue record for this book is available from
the British Library

Typeset by Seagull Books, Calcutta, India
Printed and bound by WordsWorth India, New Delhi, India

For
Abdel Azim El Wardany,
who never slept a day

Contents

∾

The sleeper's heartbeat can be timed and brainwaves plotted. Sleep can be reframed, portrayed as a psychological stage on which the tragedy of Oedipus plays out night after night. Scientific experiments might dissect phenomenal sleep and theories pick through it but sleep itself stays out of reach. It inhabits a distant, darkened corner. It participates in reality from afar, with no desire to come closer. Those who are closer cannot understand what this means, that reality can be participated in from afar. They see it as no more than stark contradiction and work incessantly to keep sleep present in their waking, which is when they look at it, brushing aside the right it reasserts each night to be present in absence. Sleep requires this work, then, because only work makes the effort to reach out and touch sleep's faint trace without trying to make it present or to convert it into an object of inquiry. Work does not seek to quantify sleep or dissect it; it wants to go to it, to visit it in the distant place where it is found. And just as sleep hands itself to work, so work gives itself to sleep, each proceeding towards the other like head meeting pillow. Because work needs sleep. Initially, work appears on the horizon as a distant possibility. The writer bends its way, trying to reach it and make it real. It becomes more unattainable. The writer persists, striving to bring it into the light. It recedes further. The tighter the grip of the force which seeks to shape it, the more impossible work becomes, and so the writer perseveres, unpicking the problems that confront him until weariness fells him and he is overcome by sleep—and at last, the potentiality of work is renewed. Only when the writer surrenders himself to sleep and the force which grips work is broken does work become possible once again. Before, work was only an image of that force; now it can return to itself. Work does not want to be made, it wants to happen, and in order to happen it must find a space for itself on the margins of the force that shaped it. Work seeks sleep because sleep is open to contradiction, to de-partition, and it can be at once present and absent, manifest and hidden, at the centre and on the fringe. Sleep and work need one another. The first wants something which it can approach without waking it, the second wants something which can forget it, and make it possible once again.

The Kingdom of Things

The room is full of its things. There is a small desk by the door and a lamp beside the bed. There is a suitcase against the wall and a flowerpot on the window frame. In the desk drawer there is a passport and a marriage certificate. In the dresser drawer, a gold earring, a bracelet. A bright shirt has been carelessly tossed over the chair and abandoned on the floor is a sock pulled inside out. We leave all this behind us and are pulled towards the abyss called sleep. There, for a moment, time stops, and we imagine that we have gone somewhere, somewhere else, but even as we arrive we are cast back into the room itself, and this time not as a presiding force but as one thing among its many, the thing which we've become in sleep propelled by irresistible sympathy towards the other things and seeping now, bit by bit, onto the pillow, then onto the bed, then out into the room. And just as we are transformed into things during sleep, so the things in our rooms transform into beings. They are not what we know. They lose their passivity and gradually return to themselves. No longer objects and implements, they are now bodies through which a hidden, inner motion flows. They are our things which we resemble and which resemble us, and the deeper we fall into sleep the more we settle into them, or they into us, or all of us together into the room. In the fraternity of sleep, we do not encounter things along the lines of power but rather in the primordial matter, in the heart of its becoming. The flood of its first forms runs through us, and in us beats a pulse as old as the universe.

The First Law

There is no escaping gravity. Things which draw away, it reels in remorselessly or holds at a fixed distance, in orbit. It sets houses, people and stars in their appointed stations; within its fields it regulates the flow of letters and punctuation marks. It lets nothing quit its control. Gravity is the force which guards the universe's order and it was in gravity's fields that life first rose up in a futile attempt at defiance. Each morning the battle of wits begins, a battle in which no effort is spared: to stand tall; to cast off gravity. Doors open and others close; some things manage to slip free and others fail; people trip and fall then get back up. And so on, all day long until night comes. A truce is brokered and for a while the struggle ceases. See the ground now, stretching out night after night like a long-forgotten truth and gathering up what drops into its lap. The ground which people cross and recross each day, which they cultivate and make bloom, which they build upon and dig into: here they are now, dropping sleeping into its lap, abandoning themselves to the immeasurable force they've spent a whole day working to subdue. Here, at the closest point possible to the ground, gravity's work is complete: the ground has received its due; its goods are returned. But no sooner is the struggle resolved than the unexpected happens: the moment of surrender, of submission, brings liberation. Surrendering to gravity, sprawled flat on the ground, the sleeper is afloat and weightless, unfastened from what draws them down and, for a brief spell, feeble sleep is a match for that great force on which the universe is founded. For the briefest spell.

The Sleeping Space

When sleep is liberated from the binary imposed by waking, when it stops playing its assigned role as an antithesis to waking or the hiatus in which waking can draw breath, then it becomes a critique of wakefulness and all the binaries which it advances. The reality of sleep is not antithetical to that of waking; it is an extension of it, a reordering. Sleep suspends gravity's pull, it confuses inner with outer, while waking restores gravity and divides reality into an exterior space which we share with others and an interior in which we close in on ourselves. Liberated, sleep seeps out from the drawer in which waking has confined it and starts to commingle with the contents of the other drawers. The space which waking establishes as separate and homogenous is, in sleep, left permanently open to interpenetration and mixing. The self, constructed as an interior space cut off from the exterior and partitioned in turn into subsidiary chambers, now seeps outside and blends with the world, and bit by bit begins to lose its inner partitions: the chamber of its secrets mingles with that of its pains, its refuge with its wilds. And the limpid homogeneity of the exterior space where the sleeping body resides is clouded by the presence of absence and brought into contact with a force which neutralizes the work of boundaries. The exterior space is no longer an architectured assemblage of the chambers and parts into which it has been divided; it is no longer given definition by the relationships between the sleeping bodies which are present in it but rather by the desires and unarticulated utterances of these bodies, whose presence is now an absence. The boundaries of the sleeping space do not reside in the geographical but in the nature of what pulses inside it. In a bedroom in a twenty-first century city: the ghosts of a twentieth-century village childhood. There are people here, shorn of their ages; desires that recognize no limits drift about. Sleep does not happen inside us or outside us. It happens when everything comes together.

The Heart of the Homes

Where did all these things come from? I stood bewildered before the heap which had been piled up inside the door to my apartment, staring, trying to identify the individual things it contained, but each time I managed to make one out it would merge into the others. From somewhere outside I heard the sound of someone breathing—the janitor I assumed—blending with the drag of his broom as he swept the stairs. The things I saw were both familiar and strange. They reminded me of the piles of possessions that had filled the rooms of my family home when it was on the verge of collapse and being vacated. Eventually, I managed to identify a small red Samsonite suitcase. And another case, a green one. The first looked like one I'd once had myself, and the second like a case my father owned long ago. Neither were faded or dusty. Instead, to my surprise, both seemed to have taken on fresh and brilliant colour. And without warning, my gaze fell on a vest which hung from the handle on the inside of my front door. For a brief moment, the vest stood clear of the heap of things which, for all their strangeness, I felt I was some part of, and I guessed that it must belong to the invisible janitor, that he was the one who had somehow brought these things here and then forgotten them. I stayed put, standing before that pile, no idea what to do with it, no clue how it had made its way into my home, now peering at it, now marvelling that it was there at all. And as I peered down, details floated ever-clearer to its surface. Here a book. There a rag. A cup. A picture. Then all falling back again into the mix. And all the while, from outside, the sound of breathing from the person I couldn't see, whose things were now run together with mine, and that sound accompanied by the sound of him moving as he swept the stairwell on the far side of the door which separated us.

The Reassured

Sometimes, the social space ceases to be an arena for negotiation and conflict, a forum for exchange and dialogue, and another, hidden aspect of the social experience emerges. Shared silence. Sleep on public transport and in public squares, in lecture halls or at work, is a twofold rejection of the social act because it takes place, not in our private bedrooms, but at the very heart of traditional sites of social interaction. The sleeper at work steps away from their work; the sleeper on public transport stops watching the roadside advertisements; the sleeper in the public square abstains from engagement. Sleep taps the public sphere with its wand and transforms it from a place of mediation and competition into one of silence and absence. Silence and absence are no longer a private matter but a collective act. Yet in its social dereliction, sleep does not make the public sphere into a place of detachment and indifference but one—how strange!—of confidence and reassurance. At the very heart of the social disruption which sleep effects, can be discerned a renewed faith in the other. One without any identifiable cause. The sleeper in public places does not bargain or compete with the other, he does not form alliances or engage. He places himself in his hands. Lays bare before him his weakness, his insignificance, his ineffectuality. Sleep in public, then, is a declaration of faith in the other, and the other in question, the other next to whom the sleeper sleeps with such assurance, is not one person but a whole community of the unknown: strangers who are there by chance; a community whose members the sleeper has no desire to know. Reassured by their collective presence, he allows himself to become, like them, a stranger.

The Delicacy of Radicalism

Bodies which travel through public places are bodies on alert; a measure of tension flows through them, allowing them to engage with their surroundings and take appropriate action. Radical acts in the public space require bodies which are tenser still, still more primed to confront dangers that may cross their path, for these are bodies which have entered into open conflict with authority, with the aim of reshaping the space. Among all the many kinds of radical act, occupation is uniquely, profoundly complex. On the one hand, it is the most extreme expression of the protest movement and its moment of greatest peril because it takes the initiative, fashioning a new reality by taking over the public space. On the other hand, it can only be fully realized by a second act of extreme, almost antithetical, vulnerability, which is the act of sleeping in the site of occupation. Sleeping while occupying is the true heart of occupation, the essence which all are seeking, and any occupation where the occupiers do not bed down in their place of protest cannot be relied on. This is why there is permanent conflict around attempts to prevent the occupiers going to sleep, because it is when they manage this that the protest becomes an occupation with political consequences. The radical act of occupation, with the clear risk it carries, is truly radical only when it sets itself aside and in its place advances apathy, an act that critiques the very principle of action. This is sleep. It is in this apathy, and nowhere else, that the power to merge public and private resides—to make the public private and the private public—and so achieve the purpose of the occupation. The radical body, tense and primed, sprawls and unwinds. Abandoning its defences, it exposes its weakness and vulnerability, and as these two qualities replicate and accumulate across the group, as weariness and pain associate and bare themselves before the eyes of all, sleep is transformed into a source of strength and a means for change. The sleepers in an open-ended occupation are no longer individuals in a battle but, lying together side by side, they become instead the brokers of a new reality, their dreams the language of this reality whose code they seek to crack.

The Principle of Hope

We bid the world farewell knowing that it will endure without us. Nothing will come to end on our account; nothing will be affected by our absence. We have done all we could but our actions are destined to remain unfinished. Now see the day, gone so soon. We bid farewell to the world and we lay our heads on our pillows. But we are not sad. We are full of hope. There, in the heart of the darkness, we find a hope quietly flourishing, growing stronger and sturdier the further we push on into the night. A hope of waking. A hope that the dark will roll away. A hope in tomorrow; in a new beginning. A hope that when we open our eyes the next day everything will be as it should be. This hope ripens inside the night like a fruit. It swells in the dark; grows sweeter the blacker the night. This fruit is sleep's gift, for sleep is the true exercise of hope; a long training in emancipation and freedom. But on what does this hope rest? On a boundless faith in the unknown, once fear in the unknown has been overcome. A faith in absence, after we have surrendered ourselves to absence. A boundless faith, in a world to which we bid farewell each night, certain we are in safe hands. A faith that arises each time we lose our control over the world;

when we entrust the world with our selves, to do what it wants with them. The hope that resides in sleep is not, therefore, like any other. It is the principle of hope. It does not arise out of a desire for a given object but from the greater desire which transcends all objects: the desire to cross to the other bank and embrace the unknown.

A Real Battle

One evening my mother stood in the bedroom of an apartment I was temporarily renting in a city far from our own, explaining to an ailing man that she wasn't able to take care of him right now and promising him that she would do so as soon as she could, while he sat scolding her. Making her feel guilty. He wore a white robe and was breathing with difficulty. He looked nothing like him, but I couldn't shake the feeling that he was my father who had died of his illness just a few months before. I was distracted, having trouble following what was going on, because I was preoccupied with making arrangements for a one-day sojourn in prison. Circumstance had dictated—for reasons that aren't now entirely clear to me, though they seemed to make sense at the time—that I take the place of one of my friends in a holding cell. I was speaking to this friend over the phone and he was telling me exactly what I had to do, giving me all the details of the cell and what life was like inside, and from time to time I would switch my attention to the conversation between my mother and the sick man before reverting to the call. I asked my friend if any torture went on and I asked him how you went to sleep in a cell, and he told me not to worry and advised me to take two sheets with me: one to cover me at night and the other to wrap around my waist. Then I remembered that I had to write an email to my employers, notifying them of my absence for the day, and as I was writing this email I saw that my mother was holding firm in her refusal to care for the man, in the face of all the arguments that he was advancing. It wasn't fear that I felt as I made my preparations, but tension. I had no intention of putting up a fight. I meant to go meekly ahead and hand myself over to a brutal authority of which I was entirely ignorant. My mother, though, was shedding her skin, putting herself in the world in a way she had never done before. She was in a real battle, summoning everything she possessed, fighting her own weakness and tenderness of heart, and on the point of emerging victorious.

Waste

History does not wait for the sleepers to wake. It is written by the waking, and only them. After all, what in all the hours of sleep is so worth recording that the history books should take it into account? Surplus hours, useless and unproductive. But these hours do not wither and fade as a surplus should. Night on night their numbers swell, become a great host. Yet a host quite unlike any other, because no matter how numerous, these hours never acquire any mass worth mentioning, nor presence. They are forever hovering in the background: ineffectual, ignored, a neglected excess that everyone knows about and no one speaks of. The years pass and sleep endures, a fine dust strewn over the pages of history, perhaps clumping here in the form of a dream, or as a vision there, but otherwise kept outside the lines, a soul which haunts everything which has not been written. In the face of this neglect, sleep offers a response: repetition. Like all essentially real things, sleep knocks the ball back night after night, creating from repetition a law. Every evening it returns to us with all its passivity and insignificance and failure, and restates its insistence on unending futility, reaffirms its affiliation with all the griefs of the past.

Expelled from history, sleep neither advances nor retreats, it does not produce and it does not accumulate, and yet, despite this, it is the line beyond which progress's arrow cannot pass. What can man-in-history possibly do, confronted by this daily waste? What can he do with all these hours of sleep? Can he cut them down? Forget them the moment he wakes? Press them down, one on top of the other, into a flaky pastry he then eats? Wander through them like autumn leaves? Abandon himself to them? What can he do?

A Breath

A single blow and all the ties that bind us to the grand ideas of our reality fall away, and we vanish from the net they weave about us. We slip free of our social status, step off the wheels of production and consumption and are cast out into the flux of matter to be made into things. Our surfaces smooth, like an orange, or a chair, or a bone. Things knit into their surrounds; they conceal no inner secret. Silently drowning in our bodies, we are restored to the limitless potential which resides in matter before it takes on form. We are returned to nature: its indifference and indifference to value. We are hooked up to the blind forces which flow through existence, the mysterious forces we spend our days vainly attempting to subdue in order to gain some relief from their brutal assaults. But does it then go away, this thing we become in sleep? If history is the account of individual selves and their occupations, then things which are compelled to silence do not stand outside it but rather at the juncture where it intersects with the primal forces which surround it: where history is open to unselfed becomings. Unlike people, things are not the captives of history. They exist within history and outside it simultaneously. In their silent language flows the past which is their only present. The thing we become while we sleep is forever slipping through the fingers of reality and making for the past. Matter breathes history, and the thing we become is no longer history's subject but its imagination.

The Time of Return

When darkness descends all return whence they came. The minute forms of *Platynereis dumerilii* pass their days at the sea's surface feeding on seaweed and flotsam, their fine hairs propelling them through the water, and then, as the sun sets, one of these hairs detects the change in the light and triggers the release of melatonin, the hormone which announces that the time of return has come. In the human body, melatonin initiates physiological changes that prepare it for sleep: steadied, even breathing; a lowered pulse; a slight drop in body temperature. In the microscopic worms of platynereis dumerlii the hormone causes their hairs to stop moving. Slowly but surely, they drop into the dark ocean depths where they pass the night. Every night for millions of years, clouds of the miniscule creatures have migrated downwards, following an unchanging pattern: in response to the darkness, melatonin flows; it stills their hairs and they freefall into the deep. At dawn, as the first rays of the sun cut their way down, the same hair is alerted to the change and ceases production of the hormone. The hairs stir and start to beat and the worms' journey to the surface begins. And a new day turns.

A Story before Sleep

There once was a fish which swam into a fisherman's net, and when the fisherman brought it out and cradled it in his hands, he saw its eye grow wide, and he asked,

What is it you see, O fish?

It said,

I see all things and I know all things.

He peered into the wide yellow eye and its fixed black pupil, and he said,

And do you see me?

It answered,

I see a poor man who labours to feed his children and works for a cruel prince.

The fisherman was silent for a while. Then he said,

My whole life I have marvelled at you fish and wondered that God created you without eyelids. How do you endure seeing all things, always?

The fish said,

The water is one great eye, and we and it are one.

The little boat rocked gently in the midst of the great lake and the fish's eye grew wider and its pupil amidst the blazing yellow blacker still, until the fisherman could see his own image reflected in it. It asked,

And how is it with you on the dry land?

He said,

God gave us eyelids, and I close my eyes to sleep and gain some relief from what I see of life's hardship and my ruler's cruelty. When I die, and close them for the final time, perhaps God will free me at last.

Slowly, slowly, silence descended on the lake, and looking into the fish's eye, the fisherman was astonished to see himself as a child, the same age as his own children, then as an old man, lying neglected in a dark corner. He saw people who resembled those he knew and he saw events resembling those which had befallen him. And the fisherman was troubled, and in alarm he turned to look at the pile of little fish he had caught, all open-eyed as they were when in the water, their faces all perfectly expressionless as they were when in the water and, now afraid, he turned back to the fish in his hands, not knowing if it was looking at him or not, and he asked,

Are you alive or dead? Asleep or awake?

And the fish replied,

We do not sleep nor do we wake. We do not die nor do we live. We and the water are one.

The fisherman did not understand what it said and his unease grew when he saw that the fish's fiery eye had turned into a golden coin, and now he saw himself reflected there with his finger stretched to pluck it out. He hesitated, then thought of all the eyes of all the other fish, and he did as he had seen. And the eye swallowed him up.

A Technique

Glowing brighter and brighter. Slowly the eyes open. Rays fall across retinas. Drowsily they roam about and, for a brief spell, memory of reality meshes with this most current impression and the space becomes both familiar and strange. Then waking begins. Walter Benjamin writes that every true waking is a reshaping of reality. He describes this waking as a technique: the reclamation of what is past, not as complete facts or truths but as a period of time that can be reshaped simply by making contact with the waker's present. Benjamin's interest is focused on sleeping and waking as collective acts. In this sense, revolution—or awakening—is to wake from a prolonged collective slumber, and Benjamin's moment of waking is the moment in which memory is shaped anew, in which the group—the masses—gradually reclaims its self-awareness through political action and becomes capable of reformulating reality, of providing an explanation of the dream in which it was caught, and emerges from collective absence into a new reality. In *The Arcades Project*, Benjamin writes, 'The coming awakening stands, like the Greeks' wooden horse, in the Troy of dreams.' Waking waits for the right moment to attack the land of sleep and liberate it. The wakers want to be freed from sleep's grasp and the only way this can happen is to invoke the incomplete past so that it might be renewed beneath the gaze of the present moment, changing both past and present. For history is not a succession of finite moments but a chain of breaks. And waking, in Benjamin's understanding, is memory's rebirth at the fleeting intersection of past and present, an instant which flares like a spark: reality ceases to be a stage on which history repeats itself and becomes a living substance in which the gunpowder of history detonates.

Coma

If revolution is awakening—a long-awaited anomaly that brings a deep collective slumber to an end—then is not sleep a return to dispossession? Is it not a synonym for failure? A failure to reshape reality? An inability to alter the circumstances of life? A defeat in the struggle to redefine the self? But a closer look at what takes place in the instant that we enter sleep tells us something different: this moment does not mark the onset of failure; it simply concedes it. It is the moment in which the sleeper surrenders to his drowsiness and his inability to remain awake. The failure comes first, whether it is the failure of the self to maintain control or the defeat of the collective in its fight for change. The moment of actual sleep comes after this: the moment failure is conceded, and is not its cause; the moment of defeat's acceptance, not of its production. The individual's sleep is the act of a self that has dropped the reins, and collective slumber is the act of a group which knows the battle has been decided and that to remain on the field would be suicide. The self which does not sleep is a neurotic self, plagued by itself. The group that does not sleep is wilful and proud, unable to alter reality because it exists cut off from it. For it to reconnect to reality—for it to gather itself again and wake—it must doze a little. The sleeper who comes to bed with unrealizable hopes soon wakes again, inspired with a new dream. The failure to alter reality is a failure that can be overcome and escaped but the failure to apprehend this initial failure and accept it is a complex failure: not a sleep from which one may wake, but a coma.

Gas

In Benjamin's view, waking and sleeping do not take place in separate worlds but are instead two distinct orderings of the same reality. Waking reshapes reality and sleep is the mirror of its crisis. In his understanding, sleep and waking operate on a single reality but in different ways. Sleep floats through reality, wanders aimlessly within it, while waking reabsorbs this same reality in order to radically change it. A question presents itself: Is sleep really powerless to alter reality? Is it concerned only with preserving the status quo? This premise is difficult to accept, since sleep is powerless to preserve anything. Sleep is perpetual loss, a lassitude incapable of establishing the weakest grip on reality, let alone preserving it unaltered. Sleep is reality's gaseous state. But although sleep is unable to offer a radical new form for reality, it can still be a match for the forces of gravity which tie it down. For a brief spell, reality appears as if suspended in mid-air and change becomes a possibility. As it wanders within reality, sleep uncouples the bonds that hold it down, making it lighter. So sleep is not an approach or technique for the production of a new reality; it is wholly uninterested in mapping the features of such a thing. Its only interest is to operate on reality by outwitting the forces that hold it down. If only for the briefest spell.

An Absence

In his Epistle, Al Qushayri relates that Dhul-Nun Al Misri dispatched one of his companions to visit Abu Yazid Al Bastami and bring back word of his condition. The man arrived in Bastam, inquired after the whereabouts of Abu Yazid, and when at last he entered his home, Abu Yazid said to him,

What is it you want?

So the man said,

I want Abu Yazid.

And Abu Yazid said,

Who is Abu Yazid? And where is Abu Yazid? I, too, ask after Abu Yazid.

Present in Truth and absent from Creation, Abu Yazid no longer knew where or who he was. And how could he, when he was absented from his senses, his heart consumed by the contemplation and invocation of Truth? For to the degree he was absent from Creation so was he present in Truth: if entirely absent, then wholly present. This is why the state of wakefulness in Sufism does not signify taking a matter in hand or effecting its change but rather a return to the world of heavy bodies, a departure from the world of airy spirits. Landing after flying. The Sufi's night is the day of ordinary men and his absence is their presence. In absence, a person is present between the hands of his lord, heedful and attentive; in waking, he returns to the created world around him and forgets Truth. The absence of ordinary men by night is the anomaly which establishes the rule of their daytime presence. For Sufis, the rule they hold to is the anomaly of ordinary men, which is absence; the anomaly from which they flee is the rule of ordinary men, which is presence.

When the man returned and reported what he had seen, Dhul-Nun Al Misri wept and said,

My brother Abu Yazid is gone with those who go to God.

Al Qushayri appends this comment:

Among the Sufis are those whose absence endures not and those whose absence never ends.

A Wondrous Device

I was walking with my friend in places that were like unto the places, speaking of Rabia and wandering without aim. He said to me that what was built on falsehood was false for sure. Suddenly, there on the road before us, stood a strange device. It consisted of two small pipes, their openings facing each other, the first puffing out dust and the second sucking the particles in after their short journey through the air. We stood and watched the wondrous device and the particles of dust shimmering through the brief moments of their passage between the cold metal mouths. The machine was cleverly made, for not a speck was lost on the way, each and every particle drawn neatly from one opening to the other and, as it went, changing colour from yellow to red to gold then back again to yellow. Yet we could not understand the machine's purpose: all it did was to move dust from one mouth to another. Did it have another purpose, one we could not divine? We stood there, astonished by what we saw. Then, gradually, we were possessed by something like bewilderment.

The Phoenix

Night dims and the journey to the lower world begins. Every passing hour of the night is a frontier that those who stay awake desire to cross. A whole world of which the sleeper knows nothing. There is the hour of delirium and the hour of insomnia, the hour of intoxication and the hour of contemplation. There is the hour of waiting at the checkpoint, the hour of flying down the city's deserted streets. The hour when clasp knives open and the blood flows. The hour when the world's pain extends limitlessly away. The day ends only for the sleeper. Those who stay awake cling to the day; they do not want it to end. Those who stay awake want to keep wandering and not go home; their home is the night and when dawn breaks they know that the journey is done and their task is complete. The day never ended but rose from its own ashes, and now they do go home, pale vampires seeking refuge from the sun's burning rays. Those who slept now wake to the new day that awaits them. They take it up: a gift outside their door, set there by a miracle.

All Night Long

The blue collars and the white, off to work in the early morning, catch sight of the brotherhood of the long night vigil still sitting up in the cafes and bars, swapping the backgammon pieces back and forth and clinking their cups. And as these passing glances fall, the city divides in two: the city of labour and accumulation, and the city of waking nights and waste; the city of future hope and the city of the squandered present. Those who stay awake rise after the wages have been allotted—no harm in missing out on what they abjure—and their daily journey begins, their quest for what is in no one's gift to give. Each night they search for a new, secret door which will lead them to the undercity where a new adventure can begin. The city of those who stay awake is not the mirror of the worker's; it does not seek to invert the order of night and day. Instead, it works to evade the hegemony of this rhythm altogether and find other cadences, escapist and distorted, cadences that are not those of labour and accumulation but rather of squandering and waste. Their city is not some alternative utopia in which they achieve what was denied them in the city of work but a vast pyre, a fire in which everyone competes to destroy anything they can lay their hands on—their ideas, their desires, their disaffection, their heart's blood—then sit contented amid the thick smoke rising.

The Language of Pain

Pain comes from the world. Sinks in like a thorn then fans out. With its sharpened point it penetrates the deepest layers then spreads through them until there is no part of the soul that has not had its fill. Pain isolates those it touches. They spend their nights caught, revolving endlessly in its orbit. Sleepless, they string together poem after poem, wander lost and raving through the night, plead and complain—all in search of the language which will allow them to converse with pain. But they do not find it. How can the sleepless detach themselves from their pain other than through a new language? A language to shatter the seclusion of their private suffering and let it dissolve into the pain of others. Then comes exhaustion: their attempts to share it with others cease and they sleep their pain; the verb of sleep becomes transitive. Their grip loosens slightly and the pain wrapped round them seeps away, returning to what it was: a part of the pain of the world. Sleep is the only language in which it is possible to share pain because when we sleep we cease clinging to it. We release it. We are not freed from pain in order to forget it, nor to keep it quiescent or ignore it. It is so we might connect our pain with a pain outside ourselves; for our pain to become the world's pain, as it was in the beginning.

In the Heart of the Night

Hearts turn to their devotions. Glad tidings come to pass. Pleas are answered. Plots are hatched. Decisions taken. Dreams weaved. Drink spins heads. The devil of poetry alights. The idea glints. Death sentences are executed. Thieves take homes. Killers sink daggers in their victims' hearts. Calm settles. The wound binds. The sick recover. Bodies tangle. Desire branches out and begins to bud. A thought shines. A son of the city goes off the rails. Ghosts appear. Wild beasts rampage in the streets. Death stands in wait. A thousand and one eyes kindle. Curses are loosed. Charms are cast. Smugglers slink. Devils goad. Angels stoop. Quiet comes. Stars shine. Prayers are answered. The city returns to itself.

The World's Back

I was standing on the roof of our old family home beneath the reddening sky, at that hour when God slips night into day, and piece by piece taking the washing from the line, leaning my body over the short wall at the roof's rim to retrieve the clothes, then straightening to bundle what I'd gathered in a pile by my side. Until I looked around, and saw that the waste ground that bordered our plot was now swamped. I hadn't noticed that the groundwater had risen so high, high enough that one could see faint ripples traced over the still surface when the breeze blew. I had climbed up to the roof, leaving behind the apartment full of people I didn't know, all chattering away in fluent English. They had taken over our home, would be living there forever, and were most of them bad people, with the exception of a young, brown-eyed woman I wanted to sleep with. I started watching the ripples and when I lifted my gaze I saw to my great astonishment that all the houses fringing the waste ground had shuttered their windows and balcony doors. Their backs, facing me, were now mute walls of redbrick, and the openings through which, as a child, I would spy fragments of other lives, were vanished. I used to see them there, leaning on their sills and smoking, gathering laundry from their balconies, beating mattresses. Those openings, at which I'd sometimes been lucky enough, as a grown man, to glimpse the shape of someone naked and lost in themselves: they were all gone like smoke. For a moment, it seemed to me as I stood there, a solitary observer of the silent walls, that I was seeing the back of the world. It sent a feeling radiating through me, a strange intimacy; not an inner sensation but an outer state. I was no longer that specific individual of indeterminate age, standing at the edge of the roof of his family's crumbling home, his mind filled with dreams and fears and desires. I was this thing shaped by the scene, this intimacy with the remnants of a world which had turned its back.

One Endless Day

Night follows day like its shadow. Day runs, to escape it. Day encircles it with its walls to contain its evil; expels it from the world of day and exiles it to another. It gives it names and epithets. Makes a devil of it. Night is now frightening, permanently distanced: a Sea of Glooms, an Atlantic which must be crossed if the safe, bright shore beyond is to be attained. And in all of this, day has no desire to know anything about night or the darknesses it contains, from which all things emerged. Day wants only to flip its page so that it might begin again, choosing to forget that without the dark there could be no new beginning; that without blotting night, day would never see how it differed from the day before. Day forgets that if there were no sleep the world would become eternal day. One endless day untouched by the rhythm created when sleep comes to complicate its course. The only description which applies to the disruption that is sleep, is rhythm. It is like walking, say, or breathing, or the pulse: a repeated movement that generates new endings and beginnings. It is a breath. It breathes in and a day ends. Breathes out, and births another.

Anonymous

Night falls and the earth turns. A world departs and another appears. In this other world, the dark blots out features, dulls edges, softens boundaries; it repairs what the lights have spoilt. By day, labour flows like a force. It toils and strives and fills the mortal elements with clamour. By night, another, quieter force is at work. It spreads its palms over the things day made and liberates them from their destinies. It returns them to themselves. At the height of day, a metalworker beats sheets, a carpenter works at a table. In the dark of night, a fruit is ripening, an idea is fermenting. Night's industry takes place under the wings of darkness and remains anonymous, unattributable; by day, the doer is always defined. As the foetus develops in the womb's darkness or the fruit swells at the flower's centre, as the worm grows in the gloom of its cocoon or the idea ferments amid clouds of intoxication, so the night: knitting its womb to shelter those who sleep. In their seclusion from the brute brightness of the lights, they are purified and made ready to enter a new day. Then morning breathes and the earth turns. A world departs. Another takes its place.

Zero Point

Does sleep precede waking or does it follow? Is waking born from sleep or does it die there? Is sleep the condition for waking or vice versa? The question of primacy seeks an origin for what follows it, a zero point from which all things begin. But what if there was no such point? What if sleep and wakefulness were not a pair of states which pass in succession through us, one springing from the other, but two intertwined bodily experiences? One experience in other words, in which the self is barricaded into the body and the body is one object among many others in the world. And then another, in which the body hides no self inside it but maintains instead a permanent openness through which it becomes one with the world. In this picture, sleeping and waking are not associated through alternation, nor do they take place separately: they pulse simultaneously through a single body, a body formed of continuous and interpenetrating experiences which will never reach a conclusion as long as the body remains alive. Experiences the body never stops entering into and never knows where in this world they will lead.

The Seventh Waking

Seventh heaven is said to be the highest height and seventh earth the foot of hell. Seventh sleep must be the innermost part of dream. What then is the seventh waking? No one knows exactly. No one has been there. Waking, for all its complexity, admits of neither mobility nor rank: it is the solid ground on which reality stands; immutable even in myth; undifferentiated, without summit or base, surface or interior. Why has waking been denied a hierarchy of degrees? Perhaps because it is the benchmark by which any change is measured. Waking is the unit which measures things around it and sets them in their place, which gauges distance or proximity. It is the yardstick that scales its surroundings and holds reality together, and its fixity cannot be thrown out by the slightest change or variation unless the whole system is to come undone. But what if, one day, waking sought to improve on its work; sought not only to measure change but to pinpoint the moment of its occurrence? What would happen if waking wanted to introduce fractions and multiples of its own strength until it became the finest of fine needles, capable of fixing on the precise moment of change and controlling it? This would surely enable it to work with much greater efficiency quantifying and categorizing reality and then to go further, to perceive in every subdivision space for another, transforming reality into an endless and infinitesimally graded calculus. And so it would go on, refining and refining, until it believed that it must be within reach of the point at which change occurs. Yet waking would never arrive at that point; would never, for example, be able to apprehend the moment in which revolution began or was defeated. In vain it would slice ever thinner, plot ever more interstitial points, constructing change from the intersection of ever more precisely delineated relationships and differentiated coordinates. And here, waking would fall into exactly what it sought to avoid: it would start to rave. In its fevered expansion, waking's states would change and change but would be unable to grasp this change. The lines of change might pierce it through but the points it calculates would evanesce and reality would no longer be the solid, immutable thing that it desires. Reality would just go on frothing and frothing, slipping through waking's fingers until it had boiled to an invisible limpidity, or until wakefulness itself had been transmuted into the purest raving. In other words, if waking extends to its full span, it will eventually arrive, after a journey down the rockiest roads, at what it had always sought to exclude from reality altogether.

The Morals of a Cat

I strolled through streets all run together and I saw that the people had changed their ways, not gathering in mass demonstrations but collecting instead in little knots whenever the traffic lights turned red; no more than five to a group, chanting their slogans and waving their signs at the junctions, then fleeing before the police arrived. The streets I went down were growing ever more tangled and, as my feet sank into the sandy surface of a street I'd never seen before, I thought to myself that while the individuals that made up each group might want to topple Mubarak, the group made up of those same individuals still wanted the Mubarak regime to survive. I began to ponder this thought, and I was still pondering it as I arrived back home, where my father opened the door and informed me that Facebook had a monopoly on photographs. The home did not resemble any home that my father and I had ever shared, yet it was a home nonetheless, and it radiated a cosy familiarity. There was a small flight of stairs brightened by flowerpots. Though I knew about his love of technology, my father's statement had baffled me, and as I stepped inside I asked him what he'd meant. He had noticed, he said, that everyone seemed to be uploading their pictures onto Facebook, even though there were other sites that were equally as good, from which I understood that he must have seen the photographs from my most recent trip. I'd put them up on the very site he himself had persuaded me to join. And I felt overwhelmingly happy and grateful to have received this subtle signal from another world. My father was slightly plump and wearing a house robe, his face swollen from the cortisone in the medication that he'd been forced to take for his ruined lungs. He was clean shaven, even-tempered. This was the first time I had seen him face to face since he had passed away the previous year, yet we were communicating as we always had. Both of us were descended from cats, you see: we couldn't take the straight line, couldn't express anything directly, but walked instead, and quite contentedly, a long and crooked path to say the simplest things.

A River Within

There is another sleep which slumbers at sleep's heart, a sleep which transcends the alternation of night and day and cycles of work and rest. We do not need to close our eyes to reach it. We do not need to shrug off consciousness to enter in. It is not a state like the sleep that orbits waking but a thin stream of distraction running through reality; a withdrawal which flows through the heart of the world. A subterranean river of abstention and renunciation. Not a rejection or a denial of reality but an integral part of it; its empty soul, without which it is incomplete. What happens, then, when this stream is given access to the cycles of production which crowd reality? What might it produce, this stream which is the antithesis of production? Nothing more than enchanted things, perhaps: a dream, or a revolution. When the stream of distraction flows into reality's cycles of production, it deconstructs them by refusing to participate and restores reality to its free-floating state: a dense flood of words and desires, objects and fluids. Reality is then a state of pure production without products, barely stable, only becoming concrete when the stream runs dry and sleep reverts to being the mirror in which waking examines itself with narcissistic passion. Before resuming the cycle.

A Call

Distraction obeys a call of unknown provenance. The call stays hidden, waiting the right time to appear, then seeps out through the holes in the net of apprehension. The individual who receives the call is carried off by a haphazard, aimless motion which causes him to slip into another world and dissolve there, to wander distracted between its threads. What does the call say to him? Barely anything intelligible, but this is how it transmits its energy: the call to distraction is a random rupture, a flaw which compels the attention. Thus summoned, the individual follows after, trying to fix on a phrase, to clarify the vision, but only moves further and further into the inexpressible, finds himself thinking of something else whenever he tries to think of something, and so on and so on until he hardly knows who he is or how he got here. The call to distraction is distractive, an instant of escape pulling behind it a long thread of such escapes. But to escape the present moment is not to leave it but to complicate it: the moment is, and it is not. The distracted are present and located, yet at the same time they are scattered throughout their unselfed surrounds. Why then don't they remain distracted for ever? Why don't they rave on and on until the moon cracks? Maybe it is because distraction is too insubstantial or fragile to endure—a fleeting, random thing, an escape from a world founded on fixity—and quickly dissolves when another call appears: a clearly traceable call this time—the call to work, to duty, the call of the state. A purposeful call, both harder to ignore and better able to command attention than those that come from nowhere.

Breaking Bonds

There is another kind of distraction: a distraction purposefully summoned. After cycles of dissolution and dismemberment, the individual returns to his self, hoping to reassemble what has come apart: a Ulysses, returned after years adrift among the islands to find Penelope awaiting his homecoming and now, his long wanderings behind him, settling at home to spend his remaining years in its shelter. The self to which he returns is not Penelope bent over her loom: in that self there is nothing to gather up, to be returned to its original state. Nor is it a point in time or a place, nor is it even a self: he returns to revisit the possibility of his departure; which is to say, the moment of his emancipation from the calls of reality and his distracted wandering through the echoes they leave in memory. Without a breaking of bonds, it would be impossible rejoin reality. Return, then, is not a single occurrence: it is a repetition. But it is not a repetition for the sake of reclaiming a fixed starting point. What our distracted individual returns to, or perpetually revisits and renews, is the possibility of leaving; the self he comes back to is simply the rhythm of coming and going, of coming together and coming apart, of bonding and breaking. If wandering is a slipping away towards the world, then the return to the self is—unlike the return of Ulysses—not its antithesis but, rather, its complement, a wandering within. In fact, there may be no distinction between an inner and an outer wandering, just wandering as one mutable or unstable motion, binding and breaking, never reaching the limit of a linear end-point but moving instead now in this direction, now in that, confusing world with self until it is impossible to tell one from the other.

Morning Sleeplessness

Rainer Maria Rilke talked about the 'inner world-space', a 'house where the birds fly silently through us, the trees rise in us, and all things are transformed into something else.' This inner space, untouched by the world outside, is not consecrated or divine; it does not require that the consciousness be emptied before it can be attained. The opposite in fact: it requires the consciousness to be full of all things, liberated from their constraints and free to transform. Consciousness, in this space, does not become a mirror on which the representations of the outer world sit reflected, but turns instead into a more transparent thing, helping it connect with the heart of a world which is frothing with transformation. Distraction is an inner space much the same as Rilke's: just this instant formed; a tiny heart the size of the world. The distracted are no longer themselves: they have slipped outside their selves. They find themselves outside their selves. Cast out from day, they are thrown into a pulsing current of transformation. Distraction is a morning sleeplessness whose sufferer is disbarred from day, the same way that the nocturnal insomniac is unable to participate in sleep. Because this inner space is a damaged space, and incredibly fragile, it is always in the process of formation. And because it is weak, easily collapsed, morning sleeplessness soon evaporates, the inner space is torn apart beneath the weight of the day's demands, and day is restored. But nocturnal insomnia drags on, long as the nights it inhabits.

A Hidden Force

Entering, we saw four small, neatly made beds set out in a row across the width of the room, and realized that one of us would be sleeping on the floor. Orange sheets were pulled tight and smooth over the mattresses, plumped white pillows shone, and though it was late, the room looked as if it had been only just cleaned. We fell to discussion and quickly came up with a plan. I offered to sleep on the floor but the others insisted I take a bed; one of them would take the floor instead. I'd met them for the first time that morning. My girlfriend had told me a group of her friends were driving to the distant city where she lived and that I could go with them. We met up in a cafe and set off. Everything was going fine and then the car broke down in a village whose name we didn't know. We each took a bed and cleared a space for the fifth man on the floor and then, exhausted, we fell into our beds. The room stilled and a faint odour floated up, replacing the reek of cleaning products that had billowed into us as we'd entered: it was the smell of sweat released from our bodies as we'd removed our heavy coats, mingled with car interior and petrol fumes. I heard the sound of someone's stomach grumbling. My heart clenched gently and I thought of my girlfriend, asleep elsewhere, and of my four companions whose shifting guts and breathing I was listening to here and now, and I was overcome by a sudden irritation that I was unable to see her, that I was spending the night with friends of hers, people I didn't know, in this village whose name I didn't know. They weren't the type who talked much but when they talked they'd lose themselves in detailed accounts of events that concerned their friends and the circles they moved in, making it difficult for me to follow. Each time one of them shifted in his bed I would be brought to, then would try to distract myself and go back to sleep. My thoughts kept wandering off down branching paths and all the while there was this feeling, like something in this room was squatting on my chest. I calculated the minimum time we'd need to cover the distance that remained. Then I was aware of shadows shifting around me and I looked up to find, to my surprise, that the beds were all empty. Everyone was up and the room was flooded with morning light. One of them smiled at me as he bid me good morning. I heaved myself out of bed and peered around at the unmade beds, the rucked sheets and the articles of clothing scattered haphazardly over them. This was another room, different to the room we'd entered by night. The night room had been full of a suppressed embarrassment; this one, still bearing the vestiges of our sleep, was possessed of a sudden intimacy. We discussed what we'd do about breakfast and in an access of enthusiasm someone suggested that as soon as we'd fixed the car we should take a tour around the district that we'd come to in the dark. And we all happily agreed.

Who Is the Sleeper?

A limb severed from the whole? A single self? A small group at rest? Those who are awake never stop belonging to a social body, even when spatial or temporal absence separates them from the body's other limbs. The traveller, for instance, remains part of the group he left behind, no matter how long or far his journey takes him. And the same with the sleeper who, despite his absence in sleep, also never stops being part of the social body. The difference between the waking and the sleeper is that the former tends to preserve his social body and reaffirm its boundaries, while the latter moves to blur the body, to muddy its purity by opening it to others. The absent individual is not a hole in an ordered social body but rather a line along whose length the whole body moves, propelled by its connections with strange bodies towards inarticulacy. And the sleeper's dreams are the moment of this propulsion, in which one body is opened to others—they are inarticulate babblings, at once personal, social and political; they are the collision of multiple desires, of clashing streams that run in all directions. Each sleeper is an inarticulate social body, a city broken free of its map, its districts and streets run together, fit not for habitation but perpetual displacement.

Who Is the Sleeper?

A limb severed from the whole? A single self? A small group at rest? If sleep is the clearest manifestation of individual agency—an act that admits of no outside participation in its performance—then the essence of sleep, without which it must remain incomplete, is the self discarding its self. Which is to say that in its most organic act, the act closest to its own will, the self does not turn in on itself but voluntarily casts off its agency, as though it may only attain itself by leaving its self. Maybe this is why we need sleep, in order to apprehend that our selves are a small group of which the self is just a part. Here, within the state of sleep, we understand just how impoverished this question is, of whether the sleeper is an individual apart or part of a collective: it is the question of a waking state which looks out at the world from the cave of the self. What the state of sleep proposes is that there is no individual as distinct from a group, and no group made up of individuals. There are only groups. There are big groups and little groups, human groups regulated by authority, groups which humans share with the dead, and trees. Through the act of sleep, which brings the self out of itself, the sleeper becomes a small, permanently open community, a group without a fixed centre. And here, even if it never ends up joining the ranks of a larger group, the individual is no abstract mathematical coordinate but a single group astir, in a state of action.

Who Is the Sleeper?

A limb severed from the whole? A single self? A small group at rest? At the heart of every group is a wound which will not heal, its pain renewed each time some part of it falls away. Yet always the group will take the side of what remains visible, will privilege the living over the dead and place its hope in the future: the hope that the wound will heal with time. The group sees in itself a history of renewal and development, averting its gaze from a parallel history of loss and disconnection. But sleep does not look away; it turns to face this parallel history head on and, impelled by the catastrophe of loss, is drawn to what is visible no longer. The eye of the sleeper is fixed on the departed; all he sees of the community to which he belongs is the absent part, the cracks and breaks which spread and widen day after day. The group to which the sleeper belongs is a lost group, marching towards the open wound. It is not cohesion that holds them together, nor looking forward, but a weakness, a looking backward. Sleep does not seek to bring ease to this wound buried in the heart of every group. It wants only to approach it.

We Set a Trap

My friend and I sat in the clinic, facing the doctor as he explained the operation to us, his assurances that it was a simple procedure sprinkled with accounts of cases in which it had concluded with complete success, cases that were far more complicated than our own. We were careful to appear satisfied, even impressed, with the doctor's claims, until the moment came and we let our fox masks fall and told the doctor that we knew that it was him who'd carried out the operation on Nadine, the one which had led to her death, and that what had happened to her was more than simple error: it was a crime. We would never stop demanding justice for her, we told him, but we knew there was no honest judge who'd rule fairly in our favour, and so here we were today to make him an offer. A compromise. He would donate half the money he owned to a charity and no more would be said. The doctor scowled as he heard us out and then, briskly pulling himself together, said that he would need time to consider the proposal. He would call us to give his final answer. Morale was high as we left the office. We had seen his face change colour as he realized he had fallen into a trap. But the days that followed brought us only trouble.

Our meeting with the doctor became the subject of misleading rumour. We were accused of betrayal for making the offer, of selling out. Everywhere we went we were met by hostile glances, insulting phrases. Tough times, full of grief and frustration, but we bore it all with patience, waiting for the doctor's final answer, for something we could bring to the others. But the doctor never called.

A Bond of Unrelation

In the brotherhood of sleep, all sleepers are equal. Their experiences, their selves, their memories, all are dispersed equally among them: even their unshareable absence is held in common. Sleep proposes another kind of community, a community that does not define the group in terms of its members' presence but as the product of shared absence: a bond of kinship that connects all those who have departed; or rather, if the expression holds, a bond of unrelation. The brotherhood is not confined to sleepers—it is not strong enough to exclude—but includes all those who cross sleep's frontier. Places, things and the dead also cross this frontier in the course of their departures. Likewise the passing hours and the sufferings that lie ahead. A teeming host, marching down the avenue of escape. But where does it go? The host has no plan; all it wants is to extend and spread, haphazard, a dust cloud which enfolds all those that pass. It includes the excluded, not to make them present but so they might continue drawing away.

A Shared Absence

There is no phenomenology of sleep, writes Jean-Luc Nancy in *The Fall of Sleep*, because sleep offers only disappearance and absence. It is not a phenomenon to be described and analysed, but an absence which answers to no analysis of any kind. In absence, the self returns to itself, and to attain this goal it must fall. The fall into sleep—in Nancy's view the necessary condition for sleep to occur—causes the self to lose control and so sink deeper. The further it falls, the deeper it sinks, the closer it comes to itself, a downward journey only ending when it ceases to be aware of any distinction between what it is and what it is not. Here, the self has reached the zero point of differentiation where all things are mixed with all things, where the self locates itself equally in everything which lies outside it and everything which lies within. It is at this this point, exactly here, when the self has cast off everything that makes it distinct and has erased the line between outer and inner, that it has returned to itself. And it is here, too, that the dead rise. In the indiscriminate, unselfed darkness that Nancy describes, far from the bright light of representation, our dead can at last appear. Now we and they are brought together by our shared absence. Only sleepers can be in the presence of the dead, for they have returned to themselves; that is, to the undifferentiated mass that precedes the self's formation. In the absence called sleep, those who have lost their selves encounter those who have returned to them.

The Hanging Garden

Who could have anticipated that the city which blooms in sleep would be the garden in which we sleepers stand like trees between earth and heaven? Floor tiles crack to reveal green shoots. Windows shatter and give out branches. Asphalt subsides and over it flows water. Buildings divide into dens and dives. Walls shift. Streets change. The city itself has cast off obedience to its masters, has entered another time, has surrendered to another power. And unlike the scurrying of the visible city, all things here happen slowly. In the hanging garden of sleep the sun's rays fall slowly across leaves, slowly the roots worm through soil, the flowers slowly open. Continual transformations, so slow that they are hidden from the naked eye. The city of sleep, at once uninhabited and seething with life: the many people who each night silently surrender to the same sleeping, though thousands of miles might lie between them, are become a garden inhabited by plants and insects and birds. Inhabited, too, by the souls of the dead. The dead flee the din of the cities of the day and are drawn to the garden's stillness where death finds its place amid the unseen changes with which that garden hums. They wander freely. They drift through the flowers, diffuse through trees' branches, pass through their trunks. We hear their whispers and they hear ours. We touch them and they touch us. We mix with them and they with us. And so we abide, till day dawns and the tiles heal and the trees sink into the ground and the buildings rise and the walls return to their places and the roads smooth out and over them flow cars. People return and the dead flee.

New Land

I buried my mobile on the median strip. We did this every time we left home and headed into the city: buried our phones in the flowerbeds facing the intersection where our little street met the main road, then headed unburdened into the city to recover them on our return. But when I got back this time I couldn't find the phone. I was scrabbling at the earth with my fingers when someone approached and told me that the authorities had come along and replaced all the barren earth along the median with fresh soil, that more was on its way right now, and suddenly there was a whole convoy of trucks driving down the main road, laden with bedding soil in which lilies stood rooted, tall as reeds. There was a smell of damp straw. The trucks were small and drove slowly, and on the cab of each flashed orange lights. We stared transfixed, my mother and I now side-by-side, and, amid the joy of local residents, who had never before witnessed such interest and concern shown to our little street, we watched as the transfer took place. The earth in which I'd buried my phone had, I knew, been mixed up with the first load of fresh soil and had now found its way to a different bed. We watched as the labourers first mixed the new soil with the old, then divided the mixture between the median's beds. We would find the phone, my mother assured me, and proposed that we call my number from hers as we walked by the beds: if it buzzed or blinked we'd find it. We began to walk down the street alongside the flowerbeds, calling and calling the lost phone, but it was no use. The road was long and there were an infinite number of trucks. Then my mother took my arm and we went over to a man to ask for help. He was the gravedigger, the man who looked after the family's plot at the cemetery. For a while we made small talk, then we asked about the gate to the family plot, to which we had instructed him to apply a fresh coat of paint, and he replied that he'd heard about what had happened at the median, how lots of people were complaining that they'd lost their things there, but there was nothing that could be done to help them now. My mother took a sum of money from her bag and handed it to the gravedigger, the way she did whenever we visited the cemetery, and we thanked him and withdrew. Then we wandered back out onto the road and stood, at a loss, by the flowerbed which faced the entrance to our street. My phone contained the numbers of all my friends and all my work texts, and that wasn't all, and the thought of losing it was weighing heavily on me. And then, suddenly, a man reared up off the ground. He had the appearance of a government clerk. He had been asleep and we hadn't noticed him. As he clambered to his feet, brushing the dirt from his safari suit, he asked if we were looking for anything. We told him our story and he said that anything found buried in the beds had been handed over to a man nearby; that he'd personally witnessed five people turn up and recover their possessions. Extremely pleased at this we asked him where this man was, and he replied that he was meant to be sitting right here. That he'd gone off on some errand and would soon be back. He made space for us beside him and we sat.

A Patch of Shadow

In a world built on holding attention and focusing our awareness, a world in which every moment can be captured, recorded and shared with others, in which every moment is material suitable for live broadcast—in a world like this, sleep is the last remaining place in which death can be encountered. Contact with the living is the presiding obsession of our waking hours but our dead stand around us, waiting for the grip of our focus on the moment to slacken that they might get through. Faced with a fixity of attention which holds them in perpetual exile outside us, they have no choice but to visit us in our dreams. Our dead don't want memorials or ceremonies of remembrance. They don't ask us to exact punishment or revenge. They don't even ask that we remember them. Our dead, their numbers swelling day by day, want nothing more than leave to remain among us, for they have no other world to go to. They tell us that the reality in which we live is not ours alone, that it is not the sole preserve of the living, for their powers operate here just as ours do; it is moved by their absent energy just as by our present energy. Our dead, whom we now permit to appear only in dreams, are telling us that we, the living, are not alive because we live in a different world to that of the dead but because we still possess the capacity to die: to cross, that is, from one state to another. Death, whose existence our jittery consciousness denies, does not take place somewhere other than this reality: to the contrary, it is death which turns its soil and brings forth the new. One by one, individually, our dead steal into our dreams. As the days pass, our absence in them grows, and their presence in us. Our dead do not want to remain in our dreams as individuals, mythical figures; they want to dissolve inside us, so that our fear is stilled and we learn how to wander and withdraw, to be free, to reclaim reality from the prison of the present moment.

Long Practice

Alongside the daily dying which permeates the hours of work and the crowded stations on the way, alongside the weariness-unto-death of the endless, empty moments and the banal expiry of the megacities, there is that other, sincerer death, proposed by Maurice Blanchot: a death which restores vigour to life and to death its glory. No thunderbolt from the sky, it is the fruit of patient effort: one must tend it so it might grow, slowly but surely, inside him. Nor is there anything to flee from: it does not mean to quit life but rather to return to the flux of transformation at its fluid heart. Still personal, it is not personified: not mine per se, but a death which was slumbering and appropriated my body. As with this death, so with the act of sleep. Sleep, when we apprehend it as an act, seems fully affiliated to a death which is incapable of stirring a single motionless thing from its place. Yet sleep is intensely active, because it changes the state of all things. Everything that enters its space becomes invisible, is liberated from the banality of clear purpose. Also like sleep, this death is a long practice for surrender: surrender to weaknesses and powerlessness, surrender to the unknown, surrender to the unselfed pool in which our selfhood swims.

Faced with oblivion, Blanchot says, we should not go in search of safety but rush to offer up our weakness, vulnerability and rapid decay: this is all that we have. Blanchot's death moves him away from calcified, accreted life and towards life-in-tempest. The more we die, the further we sink into the heart of life, awash with transformation, and are liberated from our ownership of things, or theirs of us. It happens slowly, deliberately, purely personally, precisely like sleep.

A Leap in the Air

The pictures were flying from hand to hand. We jostled over them, waiting our turn to hold them and get a closer look. We clutched them clamouring, praising this one, criticizing that, in a state of wonder as we tried to work out who had taken them. They were smooth beneath our fingers. Some in colour, some black-and-white. In each, a whole world unfolded: like a leaf of time turned and spread or the days God circulates among men. In one of them I saw myself in a river of people, wearing two huge earphones. Like the kind that come with record players. I couldn't tell if I was at a demonstration or a wedding. In another I saw Osama, erect, his weight on his left arm which hung in mid-air. The whole weight of his body on that hanging arm. His feet flown out in front of him and his right arm stretched out to one side. It was as though he had leapt in the air and the camera had captured his miraculous leap at precisely the right moment. We stared at the picture in awe, peering at it as though we might find some solution to the mystery of Osama's mid-flight pose. But we couldn't. The picture was dark, the backdrop liquid stripes of light, and then Osama, held suspended before us, his face free of the swelling that had afflicted it in the last years of his life. It was a young face, one we'd never known, wearing a pair of spectacles he'd never worn while still alive, and it was looking out at us, and laughing.

What Happens When We Sleep?

Our brows bead with sweat. Spittle runs from our mouths. A salt crust precipitates on our lips. From our bodies a faint odour drifts. A film gathers on our eyes. Our members stiffen. Our heads break open. An emptiness spreads through our souls. The ache in the shoulder fades. The cut fuses on the finger. Creases form on the right cheek. Small pimples appear on the brow. A mole sprouts on the arm. By the knee the skin splits. A muscle grows. A new memory surfaces. The bowels grow still. Blood brightens in the veins. Growth hormones flow. The hormones of exertion wane. The eye's muscles slacken. The anklebone twists. A lock greys. An idea ferments. The thumbnail sprouts. The gum parts before a fresh molar. The eyelid trembles. Hairs fall from the head. Skin puckers beneath the eye. The mood clears. Vision clears. Bile cuts a path to the gorge. The jaw muscle relaxes. A tooth cracks in the upper row. How did all these things happen? We do not know. We awoke and found ourselves this way.

The Structure of the Abyss

In the first stage, light fades gradually and the consciousness slowly withdraws. In the second, a slight drop in body temperature and the decoupling from one's immediate environment begins. In the third and fourth, the depths yawn, brainwaves slow and flatten, blood pressure falls, breathing slows, muscles relax and growth hormones are released into the blood. In the fifth, the stage of rapid eye movement, the brain wakes up, waves surging while the muscles stay slack. The eye flicks back and forth, dreams take shape and memory starts to sort its shelves. This intensity of mental activity is why the REM stage might also be termed the stage of sleeping wakefulness, and when it concludes the cycle is complete and a new one begins. Four or five successive cycles in a single night, but not all the same, their duration varying from one to the next. In the initial cycle, the pre-REM stages are longer, maybe an hour and a half, with the REM stage lasting a maximum of twenty minutes. Deeper into night these first stages contract and the REM extends, and by the final cycle, the deep sleep stages—three and four—are vanished altogether and REM expands to a full hour. The waking brain roars at the centre of the slackened body and the eye judders like a tension stretched to its limit, like potential on the brink of realization. Light's glow grows and piece by piece consciousness bobs back to the surface. The wakefulness of waking emerges from the wakefulness of sleep.

Run Dry

He asked her,

> When was this?

and she replied,

> A year ago. More.

He asked her,

> So what happened?

and she replied,

> Nothing happened.

He didn't understand. He persisted with his question:

> Something must have happened.

She didn't reply. They were side by side in bed, him stretched out bare-chested and her with her back resting against the wall. He said,

> So nothing happened. Your love for me evaporated just like that, overnight. Is that it?

Then he raised himself up so he was sitting next to her. He stared at her in disbelief. For a moment they were silent and then he said,

> I know the last while's been difficult and that I haven't tried as hard as I could to find work but I promise you, everything's going to change.

And she looked at him, and she said,

You know what matters to me is that you're happy, not whether you've got work.

He shouted,

So what happened?

and she replied, with finality,

Nothing happened.

He gazed into space and began talking:

You want to end seven years of marriage like that. For no reason.

She was on the verge of collapse but she held herself up. Her breathing was ragged. She sighed. Her eyes filled with tears and she closed them. Then she turned to him and in a trembling voice she said,

I'm looking for a reason myself. Day after day I wake up and I don't know what it is we're doing together. At first, I was frightened and I tried to fight it. I tried to prove to myself that the love was still there. But I couldn't.

Then she broke down and the flood which she'd been holding in poured out. But she didn't stop talking. Through the tears she said,

My love for you, I can't find it any more. I don't know where it's gone. I woke up one morning and it wasn't there. Simple as that. Like it was a river that had suddenly run dry.

Barzakh

I cannot move from waking to sleep or from sleep to waking without changing. When I sleep, I leave myself and become no one; waking, I find myself in a new reality. I cannot enter sleep if I do not cast my self off and hand it over; I cannot wake if I do not find my way back to reality. Insomnia is the failure to accept the change necessary for crossing over the barzakh, the borderline; it is the failure to let drop the reins and move into an unselfed world. Or is it the attempt to enter into sleep without accepting its conditions? That is, to reduce sleep to an organic function: resting the body to restore its strength. Sleepwalking is sleep's response—mocking and at the same time terrifying—to the functional logic of waking. Sleepwalkers perform the functions required of them by waking with immaculate precision—they walk and talk, engage in clearly defined activities, but remain free-floating, trapped in reality's reflections and unable to re-enter. Sleepwalkers and insomniacs have suffered a sudden loss of their ability to change and transform and are caught suspended between sleep and waking.

Seashell

Awake, a part of me is absent, lost in the folds of memory that line my present moment, then is swept away towards all that has happened or could have happened. Asleep, part of me is present: reclaiming reality from memory and depicting it in dream as I have never seen it, as though it happened differently. As though distraction were the absence aglow in the heart of waking and dream a clotted presence within sleep. Both of them—presence and absence, sleep and waking—flow through the heart of the other, are nothing without their counterpart, exactly as forgetting flows through the heart of remembering: forgetting does not cancel memory or take place outside it but is a stage along memory's journey to reshape itself through a new remembering. Responding to the cadence created when distraction and sleep obstruct the flow of my presence and wakefulness, my memory is liberated from the archive which has accreted like layers of calcium carbonate on a seashell and is once more a living creature, renewed and reborn. Remembering is not a meditation on the sequence of events that took place in the past of memory, it is the memory reborn after forgetting. First there is forgetting, a yearning for new memories, and the present moment slips away to escape the empty progression of the old. Then remembering appears, not to restore what has fled its control but to uncover a new history, of which it was not previously aware. Every morning, reality calls to memory, and it emerges from its shell to reveal itself: weak and naked as a newborn. Each evening, an exhausted memory draws back into its shell and shuts its eyes, and forgetting comes to forge new paths through it.

A Desert Island

The island is geographically tenuous: lone dot of land surrounded by water on all sides and utterly cut off from the grasping main; disc bobbing on the surface, instantly vanishing when strong winds blow. The desert island is more fragile and tenuous still, not just in its geography but in the consciousness which describes it, where, by virtue of its extreme remoteness, it is populated by the wildest and most intense extremes of the imagination. The imagination establishes the island in consciousness exactly as newly discovered territories are established on the map. There it becomes Treasure Island, the Land of the Houyhnhnms, Robinson Crusoe's refuge, the island home of Hayy ibn Yaqzan. In other words, what makes an island remote is not just the sheer scale of its distance from the mainland but also the wildness and intensity of the imagination which strives to reach it. The desert island of Robinson Crusoe, say, was less remote and outlandish than that of Hayy ibn Yaqzan's because on the former, the world of the main was re-established, while the latter opened the world to fresh and hitherto absent possibilities. Indeed, one could say that Robinson Crusoe's island was no longer an island at all, because the main had attained and colonized it, whereas Hayy ibn Yaqzan's island home held fast to its difference. On these desert islands, the tension between part and main is clear. The main, disposed to expand and reach, runs up against the island's inaccessibility and, if only for a while, is constrained to transform and to open itself to new possibilities. The Island of Sleep, the Island of Distraction, the Island of Death, the Island of Delirium, are all of them closer to Hayy ibn Yaqzan's island than that of Robinson Crusoe, for all are truly divided from reality's main. Inner islands, located at the heart of reality though separate from it. Glimpsed at the nearest bend in the road. What makes them remote is that they are able to open reality to new possibilities, those it cannot attain without changing. And because they are remote they are tenuous and fragile and soon gone. Like enchanted islands, materializing for a short span then vanishing beneath the weight of the mainland's advance which stops up every space it comes by on its way.

Power

I was given the job of following up reports that Bashar Al
Assad was stepping down. The news came out of the blue,
late one night before my shift was over, and my boss called
me up from home and told me to get on it. But I had use
a new format for the coverage. He explained what the
format was to be: small boxes laid out in columns like the
obituary page, and in each box I should place a new picture and write the next section of text. New names for
each. He told me that the initial boxes should contain
(naturally) the names of ministers, followed by editors
(his name among them, naturally) and then the rest, and
he asked me produce a draft layout of the text with the
names and pictures that were to accompany it. An hour
at the most, I said, then sat in my office, watching images
of Assad's departure on TV, the same way I'd watched the
recent departures of all the other presidents. Assad was
wearing a black overcoat, standing on a flight of steps lead-
ing up a plane, and you could hardly make him out in the
darkness, broken by the occasional flash. I was thinking
hard about the text I had to write, about the order of the
names which were to accompany the report, about which
pictures would go in which box. Maybe I should just take

some of the standard formats we used for events like this and divide the sections between the boxes: 'It is with great happiness and hope that we bring you this long-awaited news; news that will set your minds at ease and restore your faith in a brighter future, brought to you by [the names of the ministers and editors].' Then I noticed that the phone at my elbow was ringing. It was the editor, asking how things were going. Stammering, I said that I was hard at work and the layout was nearly done. As I replaced the receiver, I remembered the news formats that our former editor had trained us to use when this sequence of abdications had first begun and which we'd dropped when the new editor had replaced him. I looked at the screen and saw footage from the intense fighting currently taking place in a neighbourhood of Aleppo, followed by close-ups of Assad's face. He looked tired and confused. It suddenly occurred to me that I had never seen the new editor's face, that the only thing I knew about him was his voice, heard at a distance. And instead of getting to work on the text I'd been asked to write, I started contemplating this new format I had to work with and asking myself if the arrival of new formats and layouts coincided with the arrival of new editors—or was it with the departure of old presidents? Or perhaps the succession of formats was part of the natural order of things? Then the phone rang again. I heard the ring clearly, filling every inch of the air.

Underground

The dividing line between sleep and waking is the inner border of the state. There, power is disrupted and laws dissolve. In sleep, we are no longer law-abiding citizens but members of a clandestine society, a group that maintains an outer semblance of citizenship while within it flees underground. How alike the community we join in sleep is to sleeper cells. Sleeper cells have perceived the fraudulence and impossibility of citizenship and turned it into a facade behind which they can work against the state: cover beneath which they might pass through surveillance systems without arousing suspicion. And so with the sleeper, forever concealing himself in the folds of the state's body, fleeing watchful eyes to where they cannot find him. But the correspondence between sleeper and sleeper cell quickly falls away when it comes to their objectives. When the sleeper cell awakes—as it must, no matter how long it sleeps—the bomb which it has planted at some critical juncture of the state is detonated and its mission is complete. But the sleeper's war with the state abides. It cannot be settled by a fatal blow because it is not motivated by the transfer of power. The sleeper does not seek to substitute one state for another, he only seeks the blind spots in its body, those holes which have forever slipped out of its control.

The Unsleeping Eye

There was a kingdom of night, but gradually, under the constant assault on darkness, it was lost. Over decades and decades of artificial lighting, night was tamed and transformed from a site of hazard where rogues and evildoers held sway, where ghosts and demons disported, into a safe space free of anxiety and fear. The city's proliferating lights drove out the ghosts and converted night into another day in which morning's labours could be continued. The balance of power no longer changed with nightfall—scales tipping to favour the homeless and the brigand, then rocking back come morning towards the rulers and the rich—but now were fixed through night and day alike. The kingdom of night which had been governed by thieves, by the homeless, by the possessed and the mad and the poets, was lost, was become an extension of day, bright with artificial light, and night itself was just another work shift. Nor was this solely the product of scientific progress and technological innovation, for lamps alone would never have been unable to fulfil their mission and subjugate night without the watchful presence of the state. However bright the lights burn, the state's unsleeping eye is an indispensable condition of nocturnal security; without it, sleep would be difficult, labour would cease and all the malign powers of night steal back among us. So it's claimed. Watchfulness is the basic night-time labour through which the state first established its dominion over the rubble of night's kingdom. Then, gradually, the state's waking gaze began to extend beyond night. The unsleeping eye was not just a thing of the dark now but was present at all times, and day itself became the same artificial day into which night had previously been transformed. The eye of the state no longer had any need for distinctions between night and day; there was nowhere left outside it: nothing but one long artificial day through which all wander like somnambulists.

Emergency Law

The child can reveal what adults conceal and the madman can harm the sane, himself or others, but what of the sleeper? For what action of his does the pen hang suspended and the record stay silent? What potential for danger is there here, that exemption is required to balance the scales of justice? Does it lie in the things he might babble out while asleep? What he might see in dream? Might it be that to stray from a tightly regulated consciousness is in itself a dangerous condition, necessitating the suspension of regular laws and the institution of special legislation to take their place? Perhaps the answer lies in an examination of the principle of personhood. The pen requires there to be a person to whom it can attribute the actions it documents, and so the law—as a record of the evolving struggle between the rulers and the ruled—requires the principle of personhood. Without this principle no authority can govern, no rights can be demanded and regulated and no duties enjoined, which is why, as many have observed, the greatest penalty that can be handed down is to strip an individual of his personhood—that quality which equips him to be a citizen under the rule of law—and cast him out into the chaos of lawlessness. In other words, to declare emergency law. Personhood, then, is both a legal technicality and a method of punishment. Sleep, childhood and madness are all sources of danger because they defy the logic of the law and the principle on which it is founded. Sleeper, child and madman, each in their own way, escape their personhood, and so they must be punished by suspending the law. The suspension of the pen, the act of not-recording, shows mercy, but also carries with it a penalty: this pardon, this exemption from accountability which claims to protect the interests of the exempted, also deprives them of their rights and obligations and expels them from the state of law. In the eyes of the law the sleeper is a damaged person: not answerable for itself and, without the agency to make informed choices, unaccountable. The sleeper, like the child and madman, lives on the borders of the legislative state, outside the binary of good and evil. No pen records: the sleeper can become a child, or the child a madman. No pen records: the madman can be murdered, the child raped. And as with all emergency law, which always understands itself as exceptional, the pen is not suspended for ever. Though this temporary nature is also conditional: the condition must first change. Sleep, childhood and madness are non-essential states of being, exceptions that should not endure for ever; the law remains suspended until the sleeper awakes, till the child grows up, till the madman comes to his senses.

Golden Locks

Hani and I were in court, waiting for the verdict. Only a few people with us in the courtroom. Then the judge came in. Except for his hair which was long and golden, he looked just like the actor Mohamed El Dafrawy. El Dafrawy glanced over at the orderly and winked. The atmosphere of watchful anticipation intensified. There were those among us who were pinning their hopes on the judge finding against the army, but now rational voices made themselves heard: in the previous case, not a single charge had been upheld against a second lieutenant, so how could anyone expect a fair ruling in a case involving a captain? Hani was sitting next to me when the judge growled his verdict, which was, of course, in the army's favour. As the chants of, 'Down, down, with military rule!' began, Hani and I walked out and caught a microbus. What surprised me was that the whole way back from the courthouse I was recounting to Hani what had just taken place before our eyes, as if I was telling him about a scene he had missed in a film we'd been watching together, and furthermore, from time to time he would pass some remark which suggested that indeed, he hadn't been sitting next to me in the courtroom the whole time. Hani was much thinner than he'd been the last time I saw him, before he died, and his hair was long. I told him about El Dafrawy's golden locks and in a tired voice he said to me,

Sure, but what were you all expecting?

A New Life

One after the other they washed their hands of the victim. Declared that there was nothing else for it. That they had done everything in their power to dissuade him. Each played their own small part in the well-laid plot and the victim had walked straight into the trap. What had he done to deserve his fate? The dead man was my brother, and I was the only one of us who had realized, suddenly, the true gravity of what we were doing. I decided to save him. I armed myself with a revolver and at the last moment intervened to save him from being shot. I should have got him out of there, away from his mother—away, even, from his wife. Both of them had been involved in the plot. Right now, he should be beginning a new life with a new identity, somewhere far away. I bid him farewell without a word and he turned, stunned, to look out at his new life.

The People of the Cave

Catastrophe is the point at which the whole nature of the conflict changes and becomes a conflict of another kind, one which requires another kind of resistance. In this sense, catastrophe is not an extension of the conflict but the instant of its radical transformation, in which it loses all connection to what came before. It does not require a search for solutions or a widening of the struggle but rather a new beginning in which to create new tools of resistance—and this beginning is not brought about by managing catastrophe or mitigating its effects but by steadfastly maintaining an acceptance of powerlessness before it. This is the function of sleep. Sleep is what takes us down to the bottom which we must touch before we can rise back up to the surface. Freighted with brokenness and surrender, sleep is not a tool of resistance deployed in a conflict; it is the birth pangs of the conflict's transformation. It is the shadow of catastrophe, its doppelganger, without which it cannot recede. When the young men, fleeing the tyrannous city, take refuge in their cave, they do not set up a better society founded on the teachings of the faith for whose sake they have been persecuted, nor do they build themselves a fortress to hold against those who wrong them. They simply sleep. For three hundred and nine years they do nothing but sleep. A thousand and one suns dawn and set without the slightest movement from their sprawled bodies. Then catastrophe recedes and they wake. The cave into which the young men have withdrawn is not a centre for resistance but a place of total surrender, of a final break with the world outside. A place that can only be exited through the pains of a new birth. The sleeping group does not want to fight but, rather, to invoke a new beginning, and this beginning, emerging from the womb of catastrophe, is none other than the waking which follows sleep. Every waking is an attempt, however modest, at a new day.

The Squatting Beast

You will wake. It may take one year or one thousand, but you will wake in the end. The last thing you remember: scenes from your life all fluttering down at your feet. The cracks begin as fine hairline fractures, invisible to the naked eye, then widen into fissures, then to a run of ruptures and sunderings, until your head collides with a great ball and you are snatched away. How are you saved? And where has your life gone? Look. Look: you are not saved. You have been spat out from your life and reborn with the next morning. A part of you is forever dead. Claimed by the catastrophe along with everything else. When you open your eyes, you will find that vanished part sitting upright like a dog and looking at you. Every street you walk down you will come across it, sitting upright at a corner and washing its face with spit-damp paws, waiting for you to pass so it can look at you. You will register the beast's presence in alarm. You will long to approach it and pat it but your guilt at being the only survivor will overwhelm you. You will turn away. Then you will notice that it does nothing but sit and stare. It is waiting for you to return its gaze. One day, you summon up your courage and look. It shrinks. You will continue to walk through the streets where you encounter the beast of the past. It will continue to shrink with every glance until only its gaze remains. You will name these streets your new life. Your new life, which grows and flourishes beneath the gaze of your past.

A Strange Language

The eye of the sleeper is trained permanently on what has happened, not on what is happening. Sleep hearkens to the call of the past, forever laden with catastrophes. It marches towards them like one enchanted, like Benjamin's angel, not in order to set them right or to change them but to grant them a second life. Catastrophe, whether personal or collective, finds no resolution here; instead, its occurrence is renewed in another existence. In its attraction to catastrophe, in its reclamation of catastrophe, sleep derives a new language from the past. What is language after all, if not the capacity to extract what has happened from itself so that it might reoccur outside itself? If not the ability of words to slide and transform and escape themselves, to generate new meaning with each repetition? The language created by sleep is a strange language whose sentences endlessly slither and slide. It is, more exactly, a halfway language, a babbling: incantations and charms to invoke a second birth. Sleep is interested in the breaks which take place along life's path, not in its continuity, and its interest in the past does not spring from a desire to order history or to understand its evolution—as happens during waking—because to sleep, history is not evolution: it is a catastrophe which can only be set aside through a new birth. This new birth is waking: it will change the past but it will not repair it. Waking is sleep's hope and its future, and with every new birth the past comes back to life, not as it was but as it might have been. It mixes with the present and opens itself to the future.

The Tongue of Flame

I saw the tongue of flame flickering inside a hole in the wall
next to the electrical socket. A tiny, solitary tongue gently
asway in a small square hole, but it spoke of great danger.
I was the only one to notice it and I took off running like
a wasp-stung child to warn the others of the impending
catastrophe. I knew exactly what this tongue was: the fore-
runner of a fire that would gather inside the walls then
spring out to consume the whole house, leaving nothing,
sparing nothing. I would run from room to room, trying
to draw attention to what was happening and begging
anyone I saw to pay attention to the impending danger.
We must do something, I told them, or we shall all be
destroyed. And then I would rush back to the little hole
to see if the tongue had responded to my efforts. Each
time I returned to the flame in the wall, I would be a little
older and I would see something different. Once, I saw
the tongue of flame flickering hard as though a gale were
whipping it from within, and once I saw that it had died
away and I could not see it at all, and once I saw the wall
so hot the whole of it glowed bright red. Then I would
return to my fevered circuit through the rooms, and with
each round I made I would pass through every room I had

ever been in. Through the bathroom of the apartment where I was born, the living room of my boyhood years, the kitchen of my marital home, the bedroom where I slept alone. I saw all my relatives and all my friends and all my lovers. I saw those who'd stayed and those who'd gone. And one by one I was warning them: about this catastrophe that was rising up, slowly and quietly, out of the depths of my life.

Subaltern

From all the poses his body might adopt he selects one
and sticks to it. He stays shut-eyed as she sits by the
window, sweeping her gaze over the things in their room,
blending her presence with his absence. The sound of his
breathing, now settled and even, reaches her ears. Before
he slept, they were talking about her ex-husband and the
trip they would be taking next week. She peers at his face
in sleep, slowly clearing of expression. It no longer looks
happy to see her; the signs of surprise, of pleasure in what
she has to say, are gone. It is grown still, sunk into itself,
and she wonders if he feels love for her in sleep as he does
when awake. Is he, asleep, thinking of her as she, awake,
is thinking of him? Then the scene ends. It ends before
the character of her lover can evolve and at last give his
heart to her after endless vacillation, before she realizes
she is still in love with her ex-husband. Why is it that
sleep can't have a story? Because narrative requires character and plot, and the sleeper cannot be the hero *in
fabula*; he cannot be caught up in plainly described events.
The sleeper is a character within whom some neglected
part unfurls and piecemeal broadens, all other traits dwin-
dling away before its expressive force. No longer rich or

poor, strong or weak, woman or man, the sleeper in his sleep overspills description and description becomes too cramped to speak of him. The only accurate label is that he is a sleeper. There is no plot into which he can be drawn because the act of sleep cannot create events which evolve and grow with time. In other words, sleep has no narrative. The sleeper's waking labour is over; his stories are suspended. In this hole there is no evolution of his stories—of their love, of their work, of their family, of their struggles, of their day—but, rather, they collide with one another and entangle. The sleeper has nothing to say or to prove, and asks no one to hear him and so, when he appears in a story, it is as a secondary, passing character, one mentioned fleetingly—a bangle to adorn the tale, appearing in a scene for others to regard. Or, more harshly, sleep is replaced wholesale with dream. At this point the equations balance. Character and plot appear with the dream. The dreamer steps forward. The sleeper retreats.

A Mixture

To which category does sleep belong? To what really happens, or to what is made to happen? To the world of realities or the world of fiction? If the world of reality addresses questions raised by the present moment in order to formulate a narrative of reality, then this is not a world to which sleep belongs. Sleep protects itself from the present through absence and addresses questions through forgetting. And if the world of fiction works to create alternative realities, to author a hypothetical narrative, then this is not sleep's world either because sleep is incapable of generating any reality, let alone preserving it. Sleep's overextension, its flaccidity, means that what it grasps slips away and makes it impossible to extend the lines of any narrative to their full length. It is the site of narrative interruption and belongs not to the worlds of truth or fiction but to another category altogether: to that of poetry. Poetry is alternative fact, reality in fantasy; realistic narratives become conjectural and hypotheticals are made real. Like the sleeper, poetry is a wanderer between the worlds. It belongs to none. One world passes into the other and, in the course of this interpenetration, the poetic is given off like vapour. Hidden in the folds of the days, permeating destinies and their embodiments, poetry is released by this entanglement of the true and the fictionalized. Or maybe poetry is the very stuff of history's becoming: the sustained reworking of narratives of truth until they become altered; the never-ending detonation of hypothetical narratives inside reality. Poetry, like history, is the constant mixing of these two categories: the real and the hypothetical.

Beneath the Pillow

Beneath the pillow is an amulet. Beneath the pillow is a stone. Beneath the pillow is a photograph. Beneath the pillow is a book. Prayers and mementoes. Guns and knives. Nothing is closer to us than the things we put beneath our pillows. Just as sarcophagi contained charms or talismans to aid their owners in their journey across the underworld, so sleepers place beneath their pillow those things they hope will protect them in their journey and lead them safe to the other side. Strange journey, where only magic will serve. Like the dead, the sleeper cannot act, and so must re-establish contact with that power which is capable of direct action, a power they have almost forgotten, which is magic. The sleeper's world is kept in motion by strange forces able to exert influence both immediately and at a distance, that are able to disregard the link between cause and effect. Sleep, then, is all that remains of myth in a world cut off from miracles. Myth is the marginalized narrative, the narrative of a world which does not differentiate between waking and sleep. A narrative not governed by logic but shaped by desires and transformations. And the sleeper's myth is his salvation: giving himself up to a world over which he exercised control just a moment before. His myth is attaining the self through quitting it. But where does it come from, the magical power of things beneath the pillow? From the same source that enchanted the sleeper's body and rendered it simultaneously present and absent, alive and dead at the same time. In their first existence, things possess only their standard value in the system of exchange but as soon as they find their way beneath the pillow they quit themselves and are activated. Beneath the pillow things turn talisman: passive and active at the same time. Silently, they wait to welcome the sleeper as he seeps through to them at the onset of his journey: they mix with him and he mixes with them; they accompany him as he is drawn into the maze of transformations and then, when the time comes, they bring him safely back.

A Meadow

The sudden slope exactly where it should be at the shoulder of the cliff, the verge of the twisting road still falling away to the left. I walk without meeting a soul until I come to the Indian grocer where I bought bananas as a child. It is where it should be, on the road's right hand before it comes to the square. Back then, I would stand outside the door of the green wood hut and, after greeting him, would recite the line my father had taught me, 'Rafiq! Rafiq! Are there spotted bananas?' speaking each syllable clear and sharp, at which his incandescent gums would part in a flawless grin. A line or two in a language I couldn't understand and then, still smiling, he would hand me the bananas dotted with brown. Today, I stand in the doorway and lift my gaze in search of the Indian standing amid his meagre wares, his smile illuminating the shop's gloom, but in his place I see a meadow that spans the wooden doorframe and runs back into the endless depth of the interior. I stand there, stunned. I peer. Perhaps I might see where the meadow ends. And I cannot. As far as the eye can see there is only green, hip-height, a field of fine stalks stirred by the breeze from whose blades the sun's bright rays reflect. The meadow I see before me is no different to any other meadow I've seen, except in its end-lessness. Once more I send my gaze out, and again, that I might know just where it is this meadow leads, until at last, in the far distance, I see something that stops my mind. I see billows of light at play. Glittering over the grass. A cloud of fine shining specks, circling the meadow and tracing happy patterns over the stalks' points, the shape their gleam describes scarcely grasped before they scatter and flit to another corner. The sight overwhelms me and, stupefied, I tell myself that if the stacked wares have turned to sward then the waves of shining light must be the grocer's smile, still flowing through this place like the Cheshire Cat's grin runs through Wonderland. I do not know how long I stood there, captivated by a distant childhood now transformed into an enchanted field reaching back as deep as the distant fields where my father once toiled. Then I could no longer bear the spell and I departed the shop and returned to my twisting road.

A Daily Threshold

Gradually the day fills with events. The waking enter them, engage. Slowly but surely their minds are glutted with them, but for one small space in their heads which remains distracted, circled by cloudy fragments which they have carried with them out of sleep. Only the woken know that they have been dreaming. The unwoken cannot tell that they have left one state and entered another. Waking is the daily threshold which separates world and world, and anyone who crosses it can never be as they were before. But waking is only completed by the reclamation of dream. This does not mean clinging to it, or preserving it as witness to a past moment; instead, the woken work to bring night's dream into their day. They want to dissolve it into their reality, not keep it apart. The woken reclaim their dream by feeding it into the currents of their daily lives, by weaving it into their memories, desires and fears. Dream is not a story in a book or a scene from a film but a perpetually evasive transformative energy. This energy might be translucent and gauzy, but it possesses a great capacity for penetration, and to reclaim it means migrating from one state to another. Only the woken know that their reality is not a sequence of moments but of thresholds, and that every threshold they cross makes them into something else. And then the new day may begin.

The Daily Abyss

Gradually the day fills with events. The waking enter them, engage. Slowly but surely their minds grow glutted, except for one small space in their heads which remains distracted, circled by the cloudy fragments they have carried with them out of sleep. Only the woken know that they have been dreaming. The unwoken cannot tell that they have left one state and entered another. Anyone who fails to bid dream farewell, not even a half turn to wave before it is gone for ever, loses the chance to wake, and instead of passing from one state to another, drops into the abyss which opens with each new day. The unwoken throw themselves into the new day in order to escape their dream, only to fall prey to ghosts they cannot see, pouncing on them at every turn. Dream is only complete when it is noticed subsequently, just a half turn of regard after which it dissolves into reality and blends with other states. But dreams which remain unclaimed by their dreamers become wretched phantoms; they are prisoners of reality, and reality a prisoner of them. Like Sisyphus, the unwoken trundle the boulder endlessly: a new day begins and they look forward to a fresh slate, a blank page, but end up repeating what they did the day before. The reality of those who do not wake is a perpetual nightmare in which no change ever occurs. A single bleached moment without end.

The City on a Hill

So strong its pull, so deep the change it bears within itself, that sometimes waking can mutate into an exceptional, unrepeatable event, and be fixed for ever; transforming not into a state of constant becoming, like birth or revolution, but into a singularity in which all things are defined. This is the religious awakening. Neo, hero of *The Matrix* and one of the twentieth century's last heroic leads, gradually discovers that the reality he knows is just a grand illusion, a vast machinery obscuring the real. Long asleep, he wakes; is emancipated from the false life from which he always felt alienated and at last steps out into the truth he yearned for. And there, in this true life, he leads the fight against illusion and falsehood until he wins his victory. Neo's awakening is a religious awakening par excellence, a shift from the embellishment of illusion to the limpid clarity of truth, and in this move the boundaries of both states are set in stone once and for ever. For illusion cannot now suddenly admit the presence of a truth, nor truth allow a single falsehood to enter into it ever again. The religious awakening is a celebration of the arrival at, and entry into, the house of truth; it is a celebration of journey's end. A person may only enter into religion once; they wake into the world of truth, never to leave it. Thus Neo's awakening. It is a moment, not a becoming. It is a moment of enlightenment with fateful, unrepeatable consequences, after which time comes to a standstill and the conflict remains decided for eternity. But time does not stop, and the moments of waking through which it flows are without end and cannot be completed. More accurate to say that waking is a becoming which does not want to reach a destination: it is a revisiting that happens in all places and all the time, not a utopia or a city on a hill to be conquered and dwelt in. Who knows? If given the chance to wake again, perhaps Neo would have chosen to spare himself and his followers the hardship of their prophetic mission to reach Zion, and realized that the path to salvation does not necessarily lead where it has promised.

New Cities

In the womb of the new cities, a blighted larva grew and grew until it was a great monster, rampaging through its streets. The inhabitants, it seems, had been unaware of the larva's presence in their midst. Cars lay peacefully outside buildings and elegant towers looked down over barbed wire, the sun's rays reflecting off their smoked glass facades, ribbed and ribboning, till even I could touch in myself a kind of wonder at these edifices, mixed with grief for their inevitable fate. I walked past them until I was back in the city I knew, thinking about the larva which had grown into a monster. A whole day adrift in stupid memories then back to the new cities beside whose walls, and whose walls only, I would take my walks. And as I entered them, I knew that I had come too late, for I saw the destruction which had visited those towers, turned ruin as far as the eye could see: great mounds of stone and reinforced concrete interspersed with the still-standing shells of buildings. I walked through the wreckage until I came to a mean little hotel, its guests all single men: they looked to me like day labourers or journeymen clerks. I started to tell them about the approaching monster and they rushed outside. Then I caught sight of a friend of mine, a man I hadn't seen for decades, standing on the packed earth of the hotel courtyard. As I finished explaining about the monster, I was staring at him, and he looked back at me, a look of gratitude, then he, too, slipped outside, without either of us exchanging a single word.

He Enters a Neighbourhood

He enters a neighbourhood he doesn't know and wanders aimlessly through its streets. He encounters sign after sign. They tell him nothing. Here, though, is a bank. Here is a kiosk. Here is a chemist. Here, a government building. He tries committing them to memory, in the hope they'll help him retrace his steps, but he is so far gone now into the neighbourhood's twisting alleys that bit by bit he loses all hope of returning and prepares himself to accept the idea that he will be lost here for ever. He takes a right turn and enters a residential street. The men and women who live here are rat men, rat women. Alarmed, he hurries on to the next turning. He enters another street. The men and women here are cows. He marvels at how placid they are and starts to slow his pace. On he drifts from street to street, from alarm to astonishment, from fear to composure, until he comes to a little square, plastered with the same repeated image of a young man, and beneath it the inscription: 'Martyr of the Neighbourhood'. The picture hangs from the top of the square's lampposts and shows a youthful, faded face gazing indifferently into the camera. He looks at the portrait and wonders: Which one of us is the sleeper here? Me, walking zombie-like through a neighbourhood I don't know, or him, hanging over the square, far from the life that passes beneath him? Will my interest wake him up, I wonder, or is it his indifferent gaze that will wake me, let me leave this maze and return to history's clamour?

He Enters a Neighbourhood

He enters a neighbourhood he walks through every day.
From time to time he spies a street sign but walks on
without paying much attention: his feet know the way and
he needs no assistance. The rapid glances he casts about
tell him nothing of a place he knows so well; they only
reaffirm his hunch that he need pay no attention: there's
nothing new here to discover. The shops are open as usual,
the crowds wander by as usual, the cars edge slowly forward in traffic as usual. The owner of a corner store stands
where he always stands and robotically he greets him.
Robotically, the man responds. He has long ceased expecting anything to happen here; everything that happens,
happens outside this neighbourhood where he lives in a
perpetual state of somnambulism, barely aware of elsewhere. His eyes pick out a line of red text daubed across
a wall. It reads: 'Beware, when the monsters come . . .' He
is astonished. Starts to look around him more carefully.
He spots the same sentence spray-painted in spidery font
on a tree trunk. A few paces further on, and there it is
again, scrawled in a shaky hand across the shuttered
entrance to a shop. He knows exactly how the sentence
ends. He has seen it many times these past couple of days

in the town centre, in the wake of the bloody events that took place there. The other half of the sentence, the bit left off, should read: ' . . . lest you become like them.' Recalling this, he wonders: Who is awake at this moment? Me, strolling zombie-like through the neighbourhood I know so well, or is it the city, which rises to bind its far-flung limbs into a single sentence?

The Names

Again the quiet extends. The room which in waking had dinned with their voices is now overlain with thick silence, broken only by the sound of him turning in bed or of a car drawing past down a road close by. Nothing in the long nights bothers him more than this silence, for they never stop talking during the day. Whether arguing or making up, quarrelling or debating, what matters is that the rope of speech still runs between them. At night, she lies asleep beside him for hours and he, incurably insomniac, lies awake, unable to say a thing to her. Night after night he peers at her, fruitlessly trying to understand where she is, then, at last, is just content to watch her golden eyes skittering back and forth behind her just-parted lids. Their daily conversation is their way to love. He tells her something and she hears him, then she tells him something and he hears her; her voice vibrates in his body and his in hers. And if there is nothing to say he might contrive a fight with her over the kitchen tap, or she might tell him a fabricated tale about what happened with the neighbours yesterday. The torments of his nightly sleeplessness are doubled those times her voice emerges weakly from the heart of the long silence and starts to call.

Through the other murmurings she utters in sleep her roll call comes clearly to his ears. Names of people: some gone, others still here. Names of those he knows and those he doesn't. She calls. Ya Hanan. Ya Baba. Ya Sami. Ya Anwar. Ya Nevine. Ya Mahmoud. Ya Umm Sayyid. Ya Samia. All in the same, unvarying tone, between hope and entreaty. She does not tell them anything and she does not ask anything of them. She only calls their names, like someone summoning spirits. In these moments, the world of their shared waking is swept aside and the room fills with people. A whole world all her own spreads out within the room and he is driven out. Each night he waits in vain to be made a part of this world, but his name stays absent.

A Matter of Listening

We close our eyes but our ears stay open. We hear the clock tick in the bedroom. In the bedroom, the roar of the street. Laying our temples against the pillow we hear the beat of our hearts. And we hear the din of inner voices, ceaselessly babbling. Entering into sleep, like entering into a state of distraction, is its own unique way of listening, for it can only happen when we release our hold on the sounds we hear; when we permit them to inhabit our consciousness without glutting them with concentration. Relaxing on our beds, waiting for sleep to come, we do not sharpen our senses so we might know where the sounds are coming from or what they mean; we listen in order to forget them, to let them permeate one another. We do not listen in order to pick the sounds apart but to fuse them together, and the moment that the external sounds blend with the inner, when we are no longer able to tell the two apart, is the moment we enter into sleep, or of our distraction. It is not that the sleeper stops listening, it is that he stops attributing what he hears to a source. The sleeper is like the distracted who ignores the sounds around him, not because he doesn't hear them but because he has become a part of them. Until one sound repeats itself insistently. A name, say. Repetition captures attention; the ear shifts to another kind of listening, searching for a source and focusing on it so that it might understand the message being sent. The sleeper wakes. The distracted pay attention.

Your Voice

If it is true that power speaks the language of your thoughts and desires, that it is no longer a monster that you fight outside yourself but one that inhabits you and speaks in your voice, then your silence is the simplest way to negate its harm. Silence is the moment in which the desire for action encounters an understanding of its own contradictions. But it is not enough. The sleeper's silence may constitute the most absolute and powerful refusal to participate in the forming of a position or in the performance of an action, but in this it is still subservient to power: the refusal to take a position is, in the end, a position in itself. The only truly damaging blow against the language of destruction is delivered by the inarticulate voice. The sleeper's incomprehensible mutterings deliver the sleeper from power's dominion and confound its language. The sleeper speaks but says nothing; he only liberates a stream of words. He does not look for sentences to illuminate meaning but fragments to make it more obscure. His language is disintegrated, inverted. It does not issue from a mouth behind which stands a self. Its pieces take shape like clouds in the sky.

Tuning

Rhythm is the inner music of place. It cannot be heard with the ear alone. Everything in the house trembles gently to its beat, is compressed and shifted by its waves, even in sleep's silence. And because this rhythm—which creates the foundations of interiority and the course of life within it—cannot be heard with the naked ear, it resists apprehension, always withdrawing into the background, ungraspable, impossible to know in itself. Only when we share in it and become a part of it can we know it: in other words, when we penetrate it, and it, us. So to sleep in unfamiliar places is a serious matter. As a somatic rhythm, sleep easily connects with surrounding rhythms and returns their echoes, and the person who sleeps in a new place is subject to its alien tempo, rocked by tremors he has never known and run through by strange vibrations. Sleep is a living box of reverberation, activated by what takes place around it: synchronous and dissonant, harmonious and discordant. Picking up the rhythm of place, it synchronizes with the body's, and a drawn-out dialogue begins. No one knows where it will lead. Night after night, sleep gropes for place's rhythm, not to usher it into the arena of the audible but to keep it in its place, apart and in the background, having first caused a part of us to leak out into it. Night after night, sleep restores to us our rhythmic nature. We become strings, stirred by waves and vibrations, connecting with what lies outside us and forming new interiorities. A sense of belonging, then, is only fully realized through dedicated effort. Effort that takes place in a silence, under cover of night: a complex coordination between sleeper and place to shape a synchronicity.

Eloquence

I woke early on my day off to the sound of my phone. The caller asked who I was. The voice was faraway, unclear, and it was somehow halting and unfluent. I gave my name and the voice said that my name was on a list of people who were to be called in an emergency. That it was an emergency, and I had to come into the office immediately. Irritated, I told it that there had to be some mistake. I had no idea what list it was talking about. Then I asked,

Who are you?

The voice said,

Don't worry, I'll be there shortly.

The tone gave me pause. It reminded me of an old acquaintance of mine, a Russian I'd worked with in another department. The call ended and I got out of bed. In the distance, I could see the lamp glowing on my colleague's desk. It was pitch black and I walked until I'd reached the point of light and anxiously told my colleague what had happened. He reassured me, said he'd gone through the same thing himself. What I had to do was maintain my defences against the lack of clarity which plagued our job: so long as there were no fixed and binding rules which applied to all parties then I was within my rights to claim I hadn't known. But I noticed that my colleague, too, spoke indistinctly, that many of the words were lost before they reached my ear; I even asked him to repeat what he'd said. Then he bent back over his work and I stood silently next to him, until I found myself turning towards the door beside his desk and saw the Russian and another man walk in from the lobby. They were both fully suited, their expressions full of serious intent. When they got to me they stopped and raised their hats. I'd been right then: this was the same Russian who'd got a colleague of mine fired, a woman I had been attracted to. I looked down at my colleague, hard at work. He was paying no attention to us, so I went with the men and we walked together through the darkened lobby. I could hear the sound of my flip-flops shushing over the bare floor. When we came to my bed, beside my desk, the Russian said in his low voice,

So this is where you work!

Here is not where I am working, for as you see, I have woken up, just now.

Once again, my ears picked up distorted, choppy language, but this time it was mine. What kind of a sentence was this? I'd never heard a less natural line than, 'Here is not where I am working.' Who says that? Switching on my desk lamp and sitting down I tried to keep myself together. The two men pulled back the covers and sat on my bed. The Russian tried to lighten the atmosphere by reminding me of the time we'd worked together. The other man stayed silent. And as I nodded my head at the Russian's words, I started to assess the danger I was in.

Bliss

The paradise of the world-child which unfurls each night can only be completed by leaving it. The sleeper sinks into an abiding bliss where he supposes he shall stay for ever. A bliss which is not the bliss of the observant nor the bliss of the pious but rather the rapture of the world-child loosed from the time of his empty days and sunk in another, eternal time. This time is the past, its eternal nature emerging as the ties which bind it to the slowly receding present fall away. The past is no longer the shadow of the present moment, nor its lining; now it stands on its own two feet. Freighted with lessons and morals, invoked in every waking moment, the past severs its links with the present and summons the sleeper who is drawn towards it like a somnambulist. The past is sleep's present and in his sleep the sleeper hears its call and that alone; he sinks through its layers and folds until he is submerged. He drowns and thinks it is deliverance. But it is not that deliverance which the past's call seeks. Its call is not the siren song that bewitched Greek sailors and drowned them: it springs from the heart of all the past's squandered opportunities and frustrated desires; it looks for another deliverance. The hordes of hours lost and questions deferred and wounds unhealed return to the sleeper and forge their way inside him. But not in order to defer their own obliteration by losing him within them: they return to him only so he might look at them. Dream is this gaze. It is the sleeper being awake without awakening. It is the other present which travels the hardest roads to emerge out of the heart of the past. The instant in which the sleeper becomes aware that he is drowning in the eternal past is the instant in which the past rises up inside him and his eye beholds. And beneath this gaze, life pulses through it; it emerges from its self to become itself and for dream to take the form of a parallel history. Only when the past returns to the sleeper, not as a pale witness to what is gone but as a force which generates present possibilities for what has passed away—only then will it become a past. The past is not the memory of what is gone but a fecund present of that which refuses to pass away. And so deliverance is attained: for the deliverance the past wants is the look which lends it new life. Every night an eternity unfurls and can only be made complete by exiting it through the waking of dream. In this waking gleams a new past, a past that is yet to happen.

Starless

Unconsciousness is sleep's corruption, occurring when sleep has failed to free itself both from the binaries of its surroundings and from its assigned function: a brief dousing of consciousness. Industrial capitalism reduced sleep to a function, its task to grant the faltering consciousness a measure of relief. It regulated it as a shift, eight hours long and followed by the shift at the factory. But high capitalism, which no longer produced anything at all, came to regard sleep as a black hole. Sleep was a short swoon, a begrudged hiatus in the flow of uninterrupted communication which had to be quickly shaken off and a rapid return made to a state of contact. And as the attention economy replaces the production economy, consciousness becomes neurotic, turning endlessly about itself and fired by a promise forever unhonoured. How can such a consciousness sleep? It is constantly afraid that it might miss something, that the promise will be honoured in its absence. All it can do is remain alert until it drops into unconsciousness. Capitalism's night grows shorter and shorter until it almost vanishes altogether, and in it sleep is one long coma dispensed in doses.

The Discreet Charm of the Proletariat

Across the surface of numberless paintings and photographs they slumber: labourers and peasant women, workmen and street children. Laid low by exhaustion, laid out in their places of work or sleeping propped one against another on the pavement. The spectator observes them, some just beginning to be claimed by deep sleep, others simply letting their eyelids rest. In these paintings and photographs, the sleep of the proletariat always happens in and around the workplace, since the proletariat has no right to a place of its own: it lives in the space from which it takes its name, which is the place of work. Nor does it have the right to its own time. There is no night or day, only endless hours of work broken by snatched tumbles into exhausted sleep. What is it that attracts the middle-class spectator to the sleep of the working class? What in the sight of these bodies wearied to the point of sleep so excites them? Is it voyeurism? Cheap compassion? Perhaps the chance to exercise a self-appointed right of ownership? The sleep of the middle classes is always sheltered by walls and doors but the sanctity of working-class sleep is violated, spread out on the roadside for anyone who'd have it. The sleep of the working class which the middle classes document in their paintings and their photographs is addressed to themselves; it might excite their pity, in the best cases it prompt them to lend the workers a little sympathy, sometimes even rights, but by and large it does not speak to the sleepers. Workers have no right to sleep from an unwillingness to work, or out of idleness or discontent, nor even to sleep because they want to sleep. Their only right is to sleep wrecked by exhaustion and exertion; to remain as members of a mythic class which cannot change its conditions. The working class labours even in sleep. It labours in the images of the middle classes, both itself and its struggle reduced to pathetic subjects. Sympathies are marshalled; the status quo maintained.

An Exchange

He returns late every day. Opens the door, walks into the living room and presses the switch. The darkness scatters but the apartment stays sunk in silence. For a moment he remains absolutely still, straining to hear, then he takes off his shoes and heads to his mother's bedroom and gently pushes at the half open door. For a few seconds he stands there, anxious, listening until the sound of her breathing reaches him. Then he calls her name and waits, and she does not answer. He calls her name a second time and now she wakes. She asks him in alarm if he is there and he says to her that he is, he's really there, and she asks him has he had his supper or would he like her to make him something to eat, and he tells her not to trouble herself. He goes to his room to change his clothes, then into the kitchen where he makes himself a light supper. He sits in front of the TV, flipping the channels and eating his food, until the steady sound of her snoring comes from her room: a superimposed stream of gurgles driven by the rhythm of her breathing. The soft gurgles blend into the sound of the television. At first he focuses on the sound that comes from her bedroom, then abandons himself to this soothing synthesis. Not once has the sound of her snore come at a different time. Even those days when he arrives early he doesn't hear a sound from her when he gets in. The snoring only starts when he is sitting in front of the television. Ever since she has been on her own she has slept without snoring. Until he arrives. The snoring lasts for about half an hour. It fills the air of the room. By the time it breaks off, his body has grown heavy, drugged. He presses the button on the remote; the screen darkens and he goes to his room to sleep.

Little Heart

Striding down the street with a gun, firing randomly into the crowd: no wild fantasy, no moment of insanity, but the starkest example of the Surrealist act as defined by André Breton and one which clearly shows the great power unleashed by Surrealism's removal of the dividing line between sleep and wakefulness. This line which is the frontline in Surrealism's battle against the bourgeoisie: the movement considered the fight to erase this line to be essentially political in nature. In order to preserve the status quo, the bourgeoisie mythologize dream and reduce reality to moral platitudes; Surrealism aims to blow reality apart and fertilize it with unconscious experience, to achieve which it must be mixed with dream. This is the little heart that beats on beneath the commercialized wreckage of Surrealism. Surrealism never saw itself as an artistic movement, or not only as that. More as a revolutionary act; at least, an act in service to the revolution. And in sleep it found its politics. It found that sleep was not the equivalent of political passivity but that it might serve as a revolutionary act if dream, with all its playfulness, irrationality and peculiarity, could be remade in reality. Breton, author of *The Surrealist Manifesto*, expelled from the Communist Party in France, stated in his book *Communicating Vessels*, that the desires which move us when we are awake continue to move us when we sleep. Instead of offering dream interpretation, Breton attempts to read reality as a dream. He tells us that dream's intangible, evasive phenomena can only be read through the logic of desire; that reality can be read as dream.

A Thread

Since returning from your distant city, I see your face asleep beside me every dawn. I open my eyes just as the white thread can be distinguished from the black, and I see it facing mine. Your face, as I see it now, is no longer the page on which your features are described. The colour of your eyes is hid beneath your lids, the dusting of freck-les on your right cheek have disappeared, the small pimple that sits on your upper lip is gone. Since leaving you, I see your face each dawn beside me as I never saw it before. I see it whole and still and shut-eyed. I see it sunk in itself, self-sufficient, not waiting to be seen or spoken to. I steal a glance your way then quickly close my eyes. I am scared I will witness the moment in which yours open, because I know that as soon as our eyes meet you will vanish and the white thread will be separated from the black, forever.

The Function of the Author

In times of crisis, violent experience will sometimes find its way into dream, where it replicates, spreading from head to head and modifying itself to suit each head it comes to. During a war prosecuted by bombing raids on a city, there might be a dream about the sound of sudden explosions while out walking in the street, or scrambling for shelter through the chaos. During a wave of popular protest whipped higher by public demonstrations, a dream might come of fleeing the police and running, alone or in the company of strangers, into an anonymous building. Each night these dreams reproduce themselves and move from one person to another. A detail here or there might differ but the dream as a whole stays the same. Is this dream an individual artefact, or a product of the masses? The dreaming self claims that it is closer to dream than dream is to itself, living out dream's detail with complete emotional engagement and lining it with memories and lived moments. The group answers that it is what shapes the collective experience relived in the dream, that it is what lends dream its capacity to endure and replicate. But are dreams of discord so different to normal dreams? Aren't dreams at other times, in all their great variety, also rich with themes that can be reproduced and transferred? Falling from a height, say. Being barefoot. Deaf. Dream's origins are most likely impossible to locate; dream defies control, so it is hard to picture a specific something lying behind it. Questions over where it comes from are better answered by rejecting both possibilities. That is, dream cannot be traced back to either the individual or the group—for all that both are present in it and affect it—because it need have no author: it springs from the disappearance of the barrier between the self and the world, which takes place in sleep. The theory that its authorship has a solely human origin is refuted, replaced by a babbling that comes from nowhere at all.

Writing

I noticed that Wael had put on a little weight. That he wasn't slender and graceful the way I remembered him but had grown a little belly. Nothing can escape time's clutches, I told myself as I looked him over: nothing can halt its work on our bodies, whether living and breathing or transformed into images. Touched by time, the body— any body—will sag and stagger. Despite this observation of mine regarding Wael's excess weight, the actual fact of his existence remained marginal: like anything else you might be aware of but feel no need to examine closely. It was not the first time I'd seen him, after all. Had I really told him I wanted to read him something because I'd realized I hadn't read to him for so long? If I had, it would be the first time I had spoken to him face to face. I hadn't talked to Wael since he'd died. From time to time he'd pass through my dreams, would join their gatherings, would share food and drink with those present, would even chat with one or two of them in a voice of which only murmurs reached me, but he no longer spoke to me. Which is perhaps why my request involved my writing, because writing was the silence that we shared, as yet unbroken.

Fetishization

Dream is a piece of night which we bring back with us into day. Equivocal, like all night things, dream possesses no clear utility or benefit. Just the tremble of a distant star soon flooded by the dazzle of morning light, and fading. For which reason, the greatest danger when writing dream is its conversion into a text. That is, its consecration as literary capital and the extraction from it of artistic value. How to protect a dream, bequeathed by unknown hand, from becoming a text of the author who experienced it? How to spare it the fetishization of literary endeavour? Achievable, perhaps, if instead of working to make it manifest in the world of literature, writing goes to it there, in the world of sleep. Dream is not an enchanting scene or amusing narrative. It is a healing wound, and writing wants to touch the force which heals it. And this healing force is change, the transformation which leaves nothing as it is and by whose working all things alter and shift from state to state. This force moves towards the past and its catastrophes, then describes a world that is like our own. In this described world, catastrophes do not recur as they happened but diverge from themselves and become something else. Except that this force is diffuse and fragile, and its work is never done, and so the catastrophes never end and the wounds never heal. This force has another name and that name is poetry, and when writing abandons itself to the force which works in the world of dream it draws further and further away from the depiction of scenes and closer to itself. Closer to poetry. Now that the novel has become the law of the literary marketplace and its currency, poetry is what remains of literature in the world today, its least fetishized and sincerest artefact. Who needs a poem? There is nothing less successful or useful or entertaining than a poem, for the poem is literature's most far-flung limb, the only literary product still at peace with its strangeness.

A Second Birth

Writing down dream after waking is its second birth.
Dream as we know it requires two births to be complete:
the first in sleep, the second on waking. To reclaim dream
is no less important than seeing it in sleep; it is the process
that brings dream into the day and brings materiality to
what was psychic energy. Without it, dream flits and flies
away. The second birth can never give us the dream as was,
but like a magnet it keeps a hold on the main features: it
erects a skeleton, clothes it in flesh. It cannot of course
bring to bear the full spectrum of concentrated psychic
energy which flowed through it during the first birth. It
might indeed, at times, distort some of the details or add
new ones. The second birth is more ragged, then, but it is
inevitable because only by this birth can dream bestow its
gift. Only now can dream be explained or told; be pre-
served, even. In its second birth, dream is a child of wakefulness, as it was a child of sleep in the first. Or perhaps
it becomes an admixture of the two, a mixing that also
takes place on the other side, for the normal incidents and
events of reality—apparently unrelated to dream—only
take on weight or presence by virtue of their connection
with imagination. Only when the real event collides with

memory and is mixed with its fluids, its moist vagueness, does it gain dimension and impact. That is to say: only then does it become a living memory. In this, the apprehension of reality resembles the apprehension of dream because it can only happen through a new birth—its birth in memory—and through a transformation which ushers it from one state into another. In both instances, the second birth is as important as the first, if not more so, for it is the second birth that establishes the principle of time as perpetual transformation and change. Without it, essences would be everlasting, originals immutable. Without it, we would not know the meaning of loss and we would be frozen for ever.

An Absent Party

But we say that 'it is raining', or that 'the revolution has taken place', or that 'we have slept'. Who is it does all these things?

The rain always takes place outside—it doesn't require my involvement—which is why I can't say, 'This is my rain.' But the revolution is a collective act. I can be involved in it or not, and when I decide to get involved, I go out on the street and become a part of it, so I can say, at most, 'This is our revolution.' But sleep happens to me personally, even if I was absent as it was happening, which means I can say, 'This is my sleep.'

But the rain is a collective act, the same as revolution. We take part in making both of them, and not on our own, either, though the importance of our role might be different in each case. Plus, both of them are open to a party that is absent and unforeseeable.

Rain is highly individualistic. No drop is like another.

So is sleep, but sleep is impersonal. We don't know who is doing it. Or rather, the one doing it is always an absent party.

Sleep becomes personal after I've woken up.

And revolution becomes personal after it's over.

And my love for you?

Your love for me doesn't make me circle you like a moth around flame: it submerges me in a sea on whose shore the others all stand.

Flesh and Blood

We were sitting somewhere, it wasn't clear where, a place no different to many others. We saw Nadine walking with Nabil down a small alley which led to where we sat. They were discussing, delightedly, the small details of their day, fleeting observations about things that had happened the day before, comments on what friends had said. A normal conversation, like those that recur daily between married couples, but at the same time one that seemed particularly joyful. Nadine and Nabil were walking away from us down the alley, arms about each other's waists, and we were following their progress from behind. Some of those seated expressed astonishment at what was happening because Nadine was dead, and I took it upon myself to explain to them that what they were seeing took place every day.

Then we saw Nadine, having delivered Nabil to their door, walking back towards us. She moved with the lightness and spontaneity of someone on home ground. The closer she got the more nervous those seated became, and then she was standing before us, asking,

What is it?

Those seated glanced at one another and at last I took it upon myself, once again, to reassure them, to make them understand that the woman standing before us was not the real Nadine but an image of her. And to prove my point I reached out and grasped Nadine's arm. Contrary to what I'd expected the arm was not a handful of wind but a living limb, flesh and blood. My gesture surprised Nadine and anxiously she said,

Guys, what is it? Tell me.

All aghast now and unable to bear the tension that filled the place. Nadine standing, glancing distractedly at those seated, and those seated staring at her in astonishment. And for a brief spell we remained like this, frozen, then suddenly everyone burst out into wild laughter, Nadine too. We were in an extremity of delight, laughing so hard that we tumbled, all together, to the ground.